Easy
Elegant
Luncheon
Menus

Chilton Book Company

RADNOR,

PENNSYLVANIA

Beverly Barbour

Easy Elegant Luncheon Menus

Library of Congress Catalog Card No. 80-970
ISBN 0-8019-6831-3
Manufactured in the United States of America
Designed by Arlene Putterman

Cover photograph courtesy of the
South African Rock Lobster Service
Corporation. Featured menu appears
on page 161.

1 2 3 4 5 6 7 8 9 0   9 8 7 6 5 4 3 2 1 0

Contents

v

THREE *For the Calorie Conscious*

FOUR *Seasonal Favorites*

FIVE *Ethnic Fare from Everywhere*

Introduction

SEVEN-COURSE DINNERS may be fun, but a lunch or brunch is easier to prepare and can provide an equally elegant way to entertain friends or honor a special guest. For the convenience of the host, hostess, club manager or restaurateur, the recipes in this book have been developed in two quantities: 4 or 6 portions, and 24 portions. (Some few recipes have 8 or 30 portions, depending upon packaging of the ingredients.)

The menus themselves are divided into five categories. A section with a definite ethnic orientation is included because it's interesting to try different dishes, and we sometimes don't know what to serve with them; a selection of menus for specific seasons is provided because not all foods are available year-round.

Menus which highlight soups, salads or sandwiches are easy to prepare ahead, economical, and lend themselves readily to an attractive buffet or sit-down service, so an ample selection is included. Eggs are probably the most versatile single food we have; they are inexpensive, can be quickly prepared, and the variety of menus planned around them will surprise you.

Because most of us are on a diet at some time during the year, the section of low-calorie menus and recipes should be especially welcome.

We invite guests because we want to enjoy the pleasure of their company, but all too often the host or hostess is unhappily occupied in the kitchen. Few of us have hired help anymore, and trying to serve more than one dish requiring last-minute preparation can ruin your fun, the guests' fun, and the meal!

The answer is simple, of course: choose a menu that allows advance preparation of most of the food (the recipes in this book indicate these steps) and don't overextend your resources.

A few simple suggestions to help you enjoy entertaining at lunch, brunch or a late supper:

• Never leave more than one last-minute thing to do with each course.

• Always provide an appetizer to put your guests' appetites on "hold" while you complete meal preparations.

• When a guest offers to help, say "yes"; another pair of hands is almost always useful. But don't let your company become involved in plate scraping; that comes *after* the party.

• Honor guests by asking them to serve various courses. Have one serve the salad while another slices the bread. The next course can be someone else's turn. We all warm to our moment in the sun.

• When you're mixing and matching foods and dishes, remember not to repeat a flavor. If you're serving carrots in the stew, don't have a carrot cake.

• Every menu should involve contrasts in color, texture, flavor and temperature. A plate will be much more appetizing if both vegetables are not green, or white, or you don't serve cinnamon apple rings on a plate with Harvard beets. Soft foods should be complemented with chewy or crisp foods for a contrast in texture. Hot and spicy dishes should be balanced with bland flavors. And be certain there are both hot and cold foods at each meal; the only exception might be a cold summertime luncheon in a non-air-conditioned area.

• The freezer is the greatest help of all when entertaining, enabling you to do most of the preparation well ahead of company time. If you do a lot of entertaining, it is helpful to keep a few hors d'oeuvres in the freezer. I like to keep good breads frozen, too; they thaw quickly and make the simplest bowl of soup seem elegant, particularly when combined with a fine French cheese and celery or radishes (leaves on both, of course).

• Always include a breadstuff in your menu. Contrary to common misinformation, breads are not fattening and they certainly are satisfying. Everyone loves them, even dieters, and they tend to take the nasty edge off of impatient appetites when you find your timetable was inaccurate (or the oven was).

• Always include a dessert. Everyone enjoys some change of taste to signal the end of a meal. A chef from a fine private club in Boston once said, "The ladies say they are dieting, but just try eliminating the mousse from the menu!" There is a little mousse lover in all of us.

• A festive table contributes a great deal of pleasure to any occasion. One easy way to create a party atmosphere is with colored napkins. Poking them, unfurled, in a wine glass has become a bit trite, but napkin holders are inexpensive, interesting and easy to store.

• You don't have to have everything "all of a set." In fact, your table will be much more interesting if it isn't. One friend doesn't have two matched settings in her entire assortment of tableware. Instead, she has one place-setting of a Spode pattern which she loves but can't afford a lot of, another of her grandmother's antique French Havilland, etc. Her tables are elegant, interesting, and conversation is never a problem.

• Make a habit of scouting flea markets, auctions or antique stores for old or interesting serving pieces. Use antique sake cups for salt dishes, egg cups for liqueurs, a brass spittoon for a wine bucket, doilies or hand towels for napkins. Anything that strikes your fancy can be used somehow.

• Oriental bedspreads or furniture throws make wonderful tablecloths. So do linen glass towels; when you tire of them, they retire to the towel drawer.

• A mixture of glassware can be equally attractive—with one possible exception. Use stemmed glasses if you're serving wine. The stem permits holding the glass while you enjoy the color and flavor of the wine without over-warming the liquid with heat from your hand.

• The tried-and-true rule for serving wines is still a valid guide. White wines are more delicate and will not overpower delicately flavored foods such as poultry, veal and seafoods. Red wines are generally heavier and heartier, with stronger, more pronounced flavors and should be used to stand against heavier, heartier dishes with stronger flavors. Rosés are actually "white wines" which have been left with the skin of the grape long enough to pick up color, but not all of the tannin and body which make red wines so flavorful.

• You don't have to serve wines, nor do you have to serve cocktails. Many people prefer not to drink in the middle of the day, particularly if it is a working day. For those who abstain, have sparkling bottled water on hand, preferably with a bit of fresh lemon or lime. Don't invest in one of the imported, expensive waters (most people can't distinguish them in a blind tasting and actually prefer a plain club soda). Many of the American bottlers have recently streamlined the design of their bottles so that they make attractive additions to the bar on the table.

• When serving wine, avoid having flowers with a strong scent on the table. A true wine lover will find the flowers interfere with his pleasure in enjoying "the nose" of the wine.

• Never have candles for lunch or brunch. They were designed to brighten darkness and their effect is really lost and even appears foolish in the morning or middle of the day.

• When using fruit as a centerpiece, try to include fruit in the meal. Otherwise, your beautiful arrangement may come tumbling down when someone decides that the apple propping up the whole display is the very one he wants to eat.

• End the meal by serving a beverage away from the dining table. It allows a reshuffling of guests who may wish to speak with people who were too far away to converse with at the table.

• There are many beverages besides coffee, tea or milk, and I've introduced some of them in the menu plans. Do try a few of them, and experiment with your own ideas; just remember that the beverage must be compatible with the foods you're serving. Generally avoid sweet drinks with any food except dessert.

• When time allows, it is nice to offer an after-lunch liqueur or spirit.

3

It's easier on the host or hostess if there are glasses and bottles available and guests serve themselves. One advantage of the self-help system is that guests tend to know how much they really wish to drink; if someone only wants a taste, expensive waste is avoided.

Sharing food is one of the most satisfying ways of communicating friendship. Elegant entertaining can be accomplished easily and need not be confined to a formal dining room; a beautifully prepared meal can be transported in a picnic hamper and served in a haystack—or some other unusual setting. It's the food and your imagination that make the fun.

ONE

Superior Salads and Sandwiches

Sandwiches and salads are mainstays of the American diet. Of all of our "American" foods, these two have been refined to the point of non-recognizability in the land of their birth. The dainty European tea sandwiches with nothing inside but a sprig of watercress, a slice of cucumber or just plain butter are distant cousins of the jaw-breaking Dagwoods that we thrive upon. Even the beautiful, Danish open-face, work-of-art sandwiches pale in comparison to the "heroes" of our land.

One of the secrets of sandwich-making is spreading the bread with butter or margarine to prevent its becoming soggy. Also, never use mayonnaise if the luncheon is going to be a picnic or served outdoors, for mayonnaise becomes a perfect breeding ground for bacteria on a hot summer day.

Our salads tell the same tale. Americans like them big—filled with lots and lots of things—and well-dressed, not running about with nothing to wear but a little film of oil and vinegar. We like to make a meal of a salad; we don't eat them only to cleanse the palate.

The salad greens are the key to good salads. They should be washed to rid them of field dust and insecticides, but the leaves should be dry before they go either into the salad or into the refrigerator. Dampness turns the leaves brown, and water makes them rot.

Never dress a salad until it is ready to makes its debut. Once the dressing coats the leaves, the water that makes the greens crisp seeks its way out of the leaf—leaving the damp and sorry sight we are served often in restaurants.

Americans love sandwiches; they love salads, and they love them both together. By adding a fine dessert, you create a meal that will delight your guests.

Cup of Consommé
Molly Brown Roll-Ups
Cinnamon Carrot Sticks
Fudge Nut Pie

•

Consommé can serve as an appetizer or be enjoyed as a beverage with this unusual sandwich—ham, turkey and Swiss cheese rolled inside bread, and then deep fried or baked for a crisp crust and melted cheese.

Cinnamon Carrot Sticks nicely complement the sandwiches both in color and in flavor. Keep these on hand for emergency use as an appetizer, salad or vegetable.

MOLLY BROWN ROLL-UPS

You can bake or deep fry these sandwiches.

Ingredients	6 Sandwiches	24 Sandwiches
Bread	1 loaf	4 loaves
Mayonnaise	⅓ cup	1⅓ cup
Dijon-style mustard	2 tsp.	3 Tbsp.
Lemon juice	1 tsp.	1 Tbsp. + 1 tsp.
Worcestershire sauce	1 tsp.	1 Tbsp. + 1 tsp.
White pepper	¼ tsp.	1 tsp.
Ham, thinly sliced	6 oz.	24 oz.
Turkey, thinly sliced	6 oz.	24 oz.
Swiss cheese	6 slices	24 slices
FOR FRYING		
Eggs, beaten	2	8
Milk	2 Tbsp.	½ cup
Soy oil		

Slice bread lengthwise; trim crust from 3 (12) slices. Cut each slice in half and flatten with a rolling pin.* Combine mayonnaise, mustard, lemon juice, Worcestershire sauce, and pepper. Spread mayonnaise mixture on each slice of bread. Layer ham, turkey and cheese on each slice. Roll up sandwich; secure with wooden picks.

TO BAKE: Brush with melted butter and place on baking sheet. Bake in preheated 375°F oven for 12 to 15 minutes or until golden brown.

TO FRY: Combine eggs and milk and dip each sandwich in mixture. Fry in 375°F oil for 1 to 2 minutes, turning to brown all sides. Drain on absorbent paper.
Serve immediately.

*NOTE: For ease of handling, flatten bread between two dampened paper towels.

CINNAMON CARROT STICKS

Make a large quantity and keep them on hand.

Ingredients	6 Portions	24 Portions
Carrots, cooked	1 lb.	4 lb.
Water	½ cup	2 cups

8

Cider vinegar	¼ cup	1 cup
Sugar, granulated	½ cup	2 cups
Oil of cinnamon	1 drop	4 drops

Slice carrots vertically into thick slices either before or after cooking. Place in a glass container.

Combine other ingredients in a saucepan and bring to boiling; pour over carrots while hot.

Cool, then cover and refrigerate.

FUDGE NUT PIE

A brownie-like crust designed to cradle ice cream.

Ingredients	1 Pie	4 Pies
Unsweetened chocolate, melted	1 square (1 oz.)	4 squares
Butter or margarine, melted	½ cup	2 cups
Flour, all-purpose	½ cup	2 cups
Sugar	1 cup	4 cups
Vanilla	1 tsp.	1 Tbsp. + 1 tsp.
Eggs	2	8
Walnuts or pecans, chopped	¼ cup	1 cup
Vanilla ice cream		

Heat oven to 350°F.

Mix all ingredients except nuts and ice cream until smooth.

Pour into greased 9-inch pie pan(s) and sprinkle with nuts.

Bake pie(s) until side(s) begin to pull away from pan(s) and top(s) spring back when lightly touched with finger—about 25 minutes.

Serve warm or cold with ice cream.

TIP: The center of the pie(s) will rise during baking and fall when removed from the oven.

Bloody or Virgin Mary
Avocado Chef's Salad
Salad Dressing Superb
Sesame Bread Sticks
Tropical Lemon Meringue Soup

•

Anchovy fillets are the magic ingredient in the Avocado Salad
Dressing, and it is the dressing that makes this salad special.

The Lemon Meringue Soup is a sweet soup that can serve also
as a dessert. Some of the meringue is folded into the soup, to
make it lighter, and the rest of it floats on top. Serve it with any
kind of cookie left in your cookie bowl.

AVOCADO CHEF'S SALAD

An avocado-laden chef's salad made doubly good with an
avocado dressing.

Ingredients	6 Portions	24 Portions
Iceberg lettuce, torn into pieces	1½ heads	6 heads
Butter lettuce, torn into pieces	1½ heads	6 heads
Green onions, sliced	6	24
Radishes, sliced	6	24
Frozen asparagus spears, cooked, drained, chilled	1½ pkg. (10 oz.)	6 pkg. (10 oz.)
Cooked ham, cut in strips	6 oz.	1½ lb.
Cooked turkey cut in strips	6 oz.	1½ lb.
Swiss cheese, cut in strips	6 oz.	1½ lb.
Hard-cooked eggs, sliced	3	12
Ripe avocados, peeled, sliced and dipped in lemon juice	3	12

In salad bowl, toss iceberg and butter lettuce with green onion and
radish slices. Top with an arrangement of asparagus, ham, turkey,
Swiss cheese, eggs and avocado slices. Serve with generous portions of
Salad Dressing Superb (recipe follows).

If desired, garnish salad dressing with parsley.

SALAD DRESSING SUPERB

Can also be served as a dip—try it with fresh vegetables or with
tortilla chips

Ingredients	6 Portions	24 Portions
Eggs	2	8
Salad oil	¾ cup	3 cups
Dry mustard	1 tsp.	1 Tbsp. + 1 tsp.
Tabasco sauce	¼ tsp.	1 tsp.
Fresh lemon juice	½ cup	2 cups
Worcestershire sauce	1½ Tbsp.	6 Tbsp.
Salt	¾ tsp.	1 Tbsp.
Ripe avocados, peeled, diced	3	12
Green onions	6	24
Garlic buds, small	1½	6
Flat anchovy fillets, drained (optional)	6	24
Mayonnaise	¾ cup	3 cups

11

In blender jar, whirl all ingredients until smooth and creamy. Pour into container and chill 2 hours.

TROPICAL LEMON MERINGUE SOUP

A snow-topped sweet soup—light and luscious for a summer menu.

Ingredients	6 Portions	24 Portions
Pineapple chunks, canned	1½ cans (1 lb. 4 oz.)	6 cans (1 lb. 4 oz.)
Cornstarch	2¼ Tbsp.	9 Tbsp.
Salt	To taste	To taste
Sugar	9 Tbsp.	2¼ cups
Large eggs, separated	3	12
Lemon juice	3 Tbsp.	¾ cup

Drain syrup from pineapple and add water to measure 2 cups (2 qt.) liquid. Stir cornstarch, salt and 2 Tbsp. (8 Tbsp.) sugar together in a saucepan; blend in liquid. Bring to a boil, stirring. Cook about 2 minutes.

Beat egg yolks lightly. Stir a little of the hot mixture into yolks, then combine with remaining soup. Stir over low heat about a minute longer. Do not allow mixture to boil. Remove from heat and stir in lemon juice. Cover and chill.

Shortly before serving beat egg whites to soft peaks. Gradually beat in remaining sugar. Fold half the meringue into chilled cooked mixture. Add pineapple chunks. Spoon into serving bowls. Top each serving with a spoonful of remaining meringue.

Crab Frittata Sandwich
Chilled Cucumber and Spinach Soup
Oranges Grand Marnier

•

The frittata is cooked in an individual omelet pan and then slipped onto half of a toasted bun and topped with Italian Tomato Sauce. Make the egg mixture ahead and refrigerate.

Chilled Cucumber and Spinach Soup is a popular dish at the River Club in Jacksonville, Florida. Serve it garnished with thin radish slices and chopped green scallion tops.

At serving time, the Oranges Grand Marnier may be sprinkled with caramel crunch, or topped with whipped cream and toasted coconut. You can use this same idea with any other fruits that don't discolor when exposed to air.

CRAB FRITTATA SANDWICH

A show-off sandwich for the virtuoso of the omelet pan.

Ingredients	6 Portions	24 Portions
Alaska King Crab meat, flaked		
1 oz. per portion:	6 oz.	1½ lb.
1½ oz. per portion:	9 oz.	2¼ lb.
Eggs	5	20
Italian seasoning	1 tsp.	1 Tbsp. + 1 tsp.
Salt	To taste	To taste
Canned sliced mushrooms	¼ cup	1 cup
Cooked spinach, chopped	¾ cup (5 oz.)	3 cups (20 oz.)
Canned chopped pimientos	⅛ cup	½ cup
Egg sesame sandwich buns, 4½-inch	6	24
Italian tomato sauce	¾ cup (5 oz.)	3 cups (20 oz.)

Combine eggs, Italian seasoning and salt; beat until light and fluffy. Add vegetables and mix well. Fold in crab meat.

For each portion ladle approximately ¾ cup of crab/egg mixture into a hot well-buttered individual omelet pan. Cook over moderate heat until omelet begins to set.

Place in a 350°F oven or under broiler until center is set and edges a light golden color. Slip frittata on bottom half of toasted bun, top with heated Italian sauce. Serve open face with other half of bun buttered.

CHILLED CUCUMBER AND SPINACH SOUP

A refreshing green medley.

Ingredients	8 Portions	24 Portions
Scallions, sliced	1 bunch	3 bunches
Butter	1 Tbsp.	3 Tbsp.
Cucumbers, sliced	4 cups	12 cups
Raw spinach, chopped	1 cup	3 cups
Potatoes, sliced	½ cup	1½ cups
Chicken stock	3 cups	9 cups
Light cream	1 cup	3 cups
Lemon juice	1 lemon	3 lemons
Salt	To taste	To taste
Pepper	To taste	To taste

Sauté sliced scallions in butter until they are soft; add vegetables and stock and cook until vegetables are tender.

Transfer to blender in batches, or to food processor and puree. Refrigerate. Just prior to serving, blend in cream and seasonings to taste.

Serve garnished with sliced radish, diced cucumber and chopped scallion greens.

ORANGES GRAND MARNIER

Oranges reinforced with an orange-flavored liqueur.

Ingredients	8 Portions	24 Portions
Thin-skinned, juicy, eating		
oranges	8	24
Water	1⅓ cups	4 cups
Sugar	2¼ cups	6¾
Reserve peel of oranges	3	9
Grand Marnier liqueur	¾ cup	2¼ cups

Peel oranges. Slice skins of 3 (9) into match-thin strips. Mix water and sugar; bring to boil in medium saucepan. As it boils, drop in oranges and simmer 3 minutes. Remove oranges and place in flat, individual dishes.

Continue to let syrup simmer (with addition of orange peel) until syrup is reduced to about half.

Cool; add Grand Marnier to thickened syrup. Pour over oranges; chill thoroughly before serving.

Gazpacho
Triple Chili Tamales
Guacamole Salad
Mangoes with Cream Cheese

•

Mexican beer goes well with this menu. Strong coffee flavored with cinnamon or with Kahlua, then topped with whipped cream, is a pleasant way to end the meal (provided you can enjoy an afternoon siesta).

Prepare the mangoes by cutting along the large, flat seed to remove a slab of fruit from each side of the pit. Score the meat by cutting diamond cross-hatches to, but not through, the skin. Properly done the fruit will then be flexible enough so that you can bend the edges under and force the cross-hatching up. It makes an attractive presentation.

GAZPACHO

Hot toasted corn chips topped with cheese and jalapeno peppers make an excellent accompaniment to gazpacho.

Ingredients	6 Portions	24 Portions
Garlic, peeled	1 clove	4 cloves
Olive oil	2 Tbsp.	½ cup
Tomatoes, ripe	3 lb.	12 lb.
Green pepper, finely chopped	⅓ cup	1⅓ cups
Onion, finely chopped	⅓ cup	1⅓ cups
Cucumber, peeled and diced	1 large	4 large
Tomato juice	2 cups	2 quarts
Red wine vinegar	¼ cup	1 cup
Salt & freshly ground pepper	To taste	To taste
Cayenne pepper	Dash	Dash

Rub inside of tureen with peeled garlic. Mash garlic with a few drops of the olive oil and rub inside tureen.

Peel tomatoes. Chop tomatoes into chunks and place in tureen. Do not crush the tomatoes. Add the remaining ingredients and refrigerate for at least 3 hours.

TRIPLE CHILI TAMALES

Three kinds of chili flavor the tamales.

Ingredients	1½ Dozen	6 Dozen
Lean stewing beef or pork	1 lb.	4 lb.
Water	1½ cups	6 cups
Salt	½ tsp.	2 tsp.
Oregano	⅛ tsp.	½ tsp.
Garlic, minced	1 clove	4 cloves
Chili powder	1 Tbsp.	¼ cup
Chili pequin	½ tsp.	2 tsp.
Chili caribe	1 tsp.	1 Tbsp. + 1 tsp.
Beef broth	½ cup	2 cups
Corn husks	¼ lb.	1 lb.
Masa harina	1½ cups	6 cups

Simmer the meat with the salt in the water until well done. Remove the meat and shred into small pieces. Reserve the stock. Dissolve the three chilis in the stock and add to the meat along with the oregano and garlic. Cook until the liquid is almost absorbed.

Prepare the masa harina as directed on the package using the beef broth. Wash and trim cornhusks at both ends. They should be about

17

four inches wide and seven inches long. Soak in warm water at least one hour or until soft and pliable. When ready, shake water off the husks.

Spread about two tablespoons of the dough ½-inch thick and 4-inches square in the middle of each shuck. Put a heaping tablespoon of meat filling in center of the dough. Fold over to seal in the filling, starting with the sides of the husk toward the center. Then fold up the bottom and close with the top. Tie with string or strands of discarded husk. Stack the tamales loosely on a rack in a large steamer or covered roasting pan. Steam over boiling water for at least 1 hour or until the tamales loosen off the husk. To test, remove one gently using a mitt or tongs. If the dough comes away, the tamales are done.

GUACAMOLE SALAD

Keep covered and in the dark to prevent discoloration.

Ingredients	6 Portions	24 Portions
Avacados, very ripe	2	8
Tomatoes, diced	2	8
Onion, grated	1 small	4
Chili powder	1 tsp.	1 Tbsp. + 1 tsp.
Mayonnaise	2 Tbsp.	½ cup
Lemon juice	2 Tbsp.	½ cup
Salt	1 tsp.	1 Tbsp + 1 tsp.
Pepper, freshly ground	To taste	To taste

Mash avocados. Add remaining ingredients and stir only until mixture has texture and is not too smooth.

Cover tightly with foil or plastic wrap and refrigerate until ready to serve.

To serve, spoon into lettuce leaves.

Artichokes Byzantine
Spiced Ground Lamb in
Middle Eastern Pocket Bread
Tabbouleh Salad
Oranges and Kiwi Fruit

•

Artichokes Byzantine can be served hot or cold, as an appetizer, or a vegetable.

The pocket bread (also called pita) is fun to make—the bread comes from the oven puffed up like a balloon. It falls as it cools, but can be opened for filling with lamb and tabbouleh. If you're pressed for time, pita can be purchased in most grocery stores.

The whole secret of Tabbouleh Salad is the fresh mint and fresh lemon juice. Don't bother making it, if you're missing one of those two ingredients.

Slice the oranges and kiwi fruit and serve sprinkled with Cointreau liqueur.

ARTICHOKES BYZANTINE

Serve cold as an appetizer or salad; serve hot as a vegetable.

Ingredients	6 Portions	24 Portions
Artichokes, large	6	24
Onions, medium-size, slices	2	8
Sugar	1 Tbsp.	¼ cup
Juice of lemons	2	8
Olive or soy oil	⅔ cup	2⅔ cups
Water	1 cup	1 quart
Salt	½ tsp.	2 tsp.
Peppercorns	3	12

Cut artichokes in half crosswise and save bottoms. Put bottoms in cooking pot; add lemon juice, sliced onions, sugar, oil, seasonings, and water.

Cover tightly and cook for 1 hour over medium heat. *Do not open cover while cooking!* Drain.

Serve with juice and onions poured over artichoke hearts.

SPICED GROUND LAMB

A versatile dish that can be shaped around a spit or shaped into patties or a loaf.

Ingredients	6 Portions	24 Portions
Ground, lean lamb	1½ lb.	5 lb.
Ground beef round	½ lb.	1½ lb.
White bread, firm with crusts removed	2 slices	6 slices
Ground cumin	½ tsp.	1½ tsp.
Chili powder	1 tsp.	1 Tbsp.
Garlic, finely chopped	1 large clove	3 large cloves
Tomato sauce	2 Tbsp.	⅓ cup
Paprika	2 tsp.	2 Tbsp.
Salt	1½ tsp.	4½ tsp.
Cayenne pepper	To taste	To taste
Ground fenugreek seeds	¼ tsp. fine	¾ tsp. fine
Egg, lightly beaten	1	3
Parsley, chopped	2 Tbsp.	⅓ cup

Grind the lamb, beef and bread together, using the finest blade of the meat grinder. Add remaining ingredients and mix well with the hands.

Shape around a spit, or skewer, and broil over charcoal fire until well-browned on the outside; or form into patties or a meat-loaf shape and broil over charcoal or under the broiler until well-browned on both sides and barely pink in the middle.

MIDDLE EASTERN POCKET BREAD

As the bread cools the pockets collapse, but they can be opened for filling.

Ingredients	12 Pockets	24 Pockets
Flour	6 cups	12 cups
Salt	1 Tbsp.	2 Tbsp.
Sugar	2 Tbsp. + 1 tsp.	¼ cup + 2 tsp.
Dry active yeast	1 package	2 packages
Water, lukewarm	2½ to 3 cups	5 to 6 cups

Place the flour, salt and 2 (4) Tbsp. sugar in a large bowl. In a small bowl mix the remaining sugar, yeast and ½ (1) cup of water. Set in a warm place until bubbly, about 10 minutes.

Stir the yeast mixture and enough warm water into the flour mixture to make a soft dough. The dough should be slightly sticky on the outside. Knead the dough until it is smooth and satiny, at least 10 minutes. It loses the stickiness quickly.

Place dough in clean bowl. Grease the top of the dough with oil, cover the bowl and set in a warm place to rise until doubled in bulk, about 1¼ hours. Punch the dough down, knead briefly, divide into 12 (24) equal pieces. Form each into a smooth ball, cover and let stand 10 minutes.

Preheat oven to 450°F.

Roll out the balls of dough into rounds about five inches in diameter. If you are using a gas oven, slide the rounds of dough directly onto the bottom of the oven. Four will fit in the average oven at one time. Bake eight minutes or until well-puffed and lightly browned. Alternately they may be placed on ungreased baking sheets and baked eight to ten minutes. If tops are pale, place under the broiler briefly.

Cool on a board covered with a towel.

TABBOULEH SALAD

Mint and lemon are the predominant flavors in this refreshing dish.

Ingredients	6 Portions	24 Portions
Bulghur, fine	1 cup	4 cups
Parsley, finely chopped	2 cups	8 cups

Green onions, finely chopped	½ cup	2 cups
Mint, fresh, chopped	½ cup	2 cups
Lemon juice	¼ cup	1 cup
Allspice	1 tsp.	1 Tbsp. + 1 tsp.
Salt	½ tsp.	2 tsp.
Black pepper	¼ tsp.	1 tsp.
Romaine	1 head	4 heads
Olive oil	¼ cup	1 cup
Tomatoes, peeled and finely chopped	3 ripe	12 ripe

Soak bulghur in cold water to cover for 1 hour. Drain and place on cloth napkin or cheesecloth and squeeze out moisture. Mix with parsley. Toss with onions, mint, lemon juice, allspice, salt and black pepper. Refrigerate.

Wash and separate leaves of romaine. Dry, wrap in towel and refrigerate.

Just before serving, toss into bulghur mixture the olive oil and tomatoes. Place some of the romaine leaves on a serving platter and mound bulghur mixture on top. Surround with remaining leaves which may be used to scoop up the tabbouleh. Garnish with lemon and tomato wedges.

Mini-Loaf Whole Wheat Bread
Shrimp and Pineapple Salad
Individual Coffee Walnut Soufflés

•

Tarragon dressing gives this salad plate with shrimp, hard-cooked egg, asparagus and pineapple rings the taste appeal to match its eye appeal.

But it's the cold soufflés that are really spectacular, particularly if you make them in straight-sided wine glasses with aluminum foil collars so that the dessert sets well above the rim of the glass.

SHRIMP AND PINEAPPLE SALAD

This salad is a year-round favorite.

Ingredients	4 Portions	24 Portions
Shrimp, large (26–30 count)	1 lb.	6 lb.
Asparagus, large spears, trimmed 4 to 5 inches	⅔ lb.	4 lb.
Leaf lettuce	For garnish	For garnish
Iceberg lettuce, shredded	½ lb.	3 lb.
Eggs, hard-cooked, halved	2	12
Pineapple, canned slices	8	48
Lemons, cut in wedges	⅔	4
Parsley sprigs	4	24

Cook shrimp; remove shells, leaving tails on, and chill.

Cook asparagus 5 to 8 minutes, until tender-crisp. Drain and chill.

Line serving platters with leaf lettuce. Add 2 oz. (1 cup) shredded iceberg lettuce to each. Arrange 2½ oz. shrimp (about 6), 2½ oz. asparagus spears (4 to 5), ½ hard-cooked egg, and 2 well-drained pineapple slices on each. Garnish with lemon wedge and parsley sprig. Serve *Tarragon Dressing* on the side.

TARRAGON DRESSING

Ingredients	2⅔ Cups	4 Quarts
Soy oil	1⅓ cup	2 quarts
Tarragon white wine vinegar	1⅓ cup	2 quarts
Lemon juice	2 Tbsp.	⅔ cup
Salt	⅔ tsp.	4 tsp.
Dry mustard	⅔ tsp.	4 tsp.
Paprika	1 tsp.	1 Tbsp.
Onion, chopped	½ tsp.	1 Tbsp.
Basil, finely crumbled	¼ tsp.	1½ tsp.

Combine all ingredients; mix well. Stir well before serving.

INDIVIDUAL COFFEE WALNUT SOUFFLÉS

May be served in glasses, molded in any attractive mold, or turned into baked pie shells.

Ingredients	6 Portions	24 Portions
Gelatin, unflavored	1 envelope	4 envelopes
Sugar	½ cup, divided	2 cups, divided

Instant coffee powder	2 Tbsp.	½ cup
Salt	Dash	½ tsp.
Eggs, separated	2	8
Milk	1¼ cup	5 cups
Vanilla extract	½ tsp.	2 tsp.
Heavy cream	1 cup	1 quart
Walnuts, finely chopped	¼ cup	1 cup

Combine gelatin, half of the sugar, instant coffee and salt in 1-quart (4-quart) saucepan. Beat egg yolks with milk. Add to gelatin mixture. Stir over low heat until gelatin dissolves and mixture thickens slightly: about 10 to 12 minutes. Remove from heat; add vanilla. Chill, stirring occasionally, until mixture mounds slightly when dropped from spoon.

Meanwhile, prepare collars on dessert glasses by binding a double strip of aluminum foil firmly around top of each glass extending 1 inch above top rim.

Beat egg whites until stiff, but not dry. Add remaining sugar gradually. Beat until very stiff. Fold in gelatin mixture. Whip cream; fold into gelatin mixture, along with walnuts. Spoon into prepared dessert glasses. Chill until firm.

Remove collars. Garnish with additional chopped walnuts, if desired.

Carrot Soup
Bacon-Cheese Wafflewich
Cinnamon Apple Sauce
Chocolate Pecan Sponge Cake

•

Soup is good but soup and sandwiches are even better—particularly in the fall. Add a Bacon-Cheese Wafflewich to the Carrot Soup and you have a winning meal—one that is unusual enough to intrigue any guests who may frequent your table

Carrot Soup is a big favorite with gardeners, and there is no reason why they should have all the pleasure for themselves. Carrots are so inexpensive to buy that the soup is a real budget stretcher—full of vitamin A, too.

The Chocolate Pecan Sponge Cake is picture-pretty when baked in a Bundt pan, or any tube pan. This cake can even be frozen wearing frosting.

CARROT SOUP

Much like a potato soup but with a more attractive color.

Ingredients	6 Portions	24 Portions
Carrots, sliced raw	2 cups	8 cups
Onion, chopped	1 medium-size	4 medium-size
Flour	¼ cup	1 cup
Butter	1 Tbsp.	4 Tbsp.
Salt	2 tsp.	2 Tbsp. + 2 tsp.
Pepper	¼ tsp.	1 tsp.
Dill seed	¼ tsp.	1 tsp.
Milk	1 quart	4 quarts
Chopped parsley or mint		

Place scraped, sliced carrots in saucepan with chopped onion and water. Simmer until carrots are very tender. Drain and puree carrots and onion in blender or food processor.

Return to saucepan and stir in flour, butter, salt, pepper and dill seed. Gradually blend in milk, stirring smooth. Heat, stirring constantly, until soup reaches boiling point.

Serve piping hot with sprinkling of chopped parsley or mint for garnish.

BACON-CHEESE WAFFLEWICH

Waffles freeze well and here is a spot to use any you've made ahead. Or, buy the frozen product.

Ingredients	4 Sandwiches	24 Sandwiches
Bacon or ham, sliced	¼ lb.	1½ lb.
Swiss cheese, sliced	¼ lb.	1½ lb.
Horseradish	½ Tbsp.	3 Tbsp.
Mayonnaise	½ Tbsp.	3 Tbsp.
Dijon mustard	½ Tbsp.	3 Tbsp.
Waffles	2	12
Tomato	4 slices	24 slices

Cut bacon slices in half. Fry until crisp.

Blend together horseradish, mayonnaise and mustard.

Split each waffle into quarters. Top each of quarters with 2 half slices bacon, cheese slice, tomato slice and some horseradish sauce. Close with remaining waffle quarters.

Cut in half for serving.

CHOCOLATE PECAN SPONGE CAKE

The name says it all!

Ingredients	1 Cake (1 10" Bundt pan)	2 Cakes (2 10" Bundt pans)
Water	1¼ cups	2½ cups
Semi-sweet chocolate pieces	1 cup (6 oz.)	2 cups (12 oz.)
Instant coffee	2 tsp.	1 Tbsp. + 1 tsp.
Flour, unsifted	1¾ cups	3½ cups
Baking soda	1½ tsp.	1 Tbsp.
Salt	1 tsp.	2 tsp.
Eggs	6	12
Vanilla extract	1 tsp.	2 tsp.
Pecans, chopped	½ cup	1 cup

Preheat oven to 350°F.

Combine over hot (not boiling) water: semi-sweet chocolate pieces and instant coffee; stir until pieces melt and mixture is smooth. Remove from heat and set aside.

In small bowl, combine flour, baking soda and salt; set aside. In large bowl, combine eggs and vanilla extract. Gradually beat in sugar; beat 5 minutes at high speed until very thick. Alternately add flour mixture with chocolate mixture. Fold in pecans. Pour into greased pan(s). Bake for 1 hour and 10 minutes.

Cool 10 minutes, remove from pan. Cool completely. Drizzle top with *Glaze* (recipe follows). Serve with chocolate ice cream.

GLAZE

Ingredients	1 Cake	2 Cakes
Confectioners' sugar, sifted	1 cup	2 cups
Water	4 tsp.	2 Tbsp. + 2 tsp.
Vanilla extract	½ tsp.	1 tsp.

In small bowl, combine confectioners' sugar, water and vanilla extract; mix thoroughly.

Salad-on-a-Skewer
Assorted Cheeses
Toasted Crackers
Rum Rice Pudding with Rum Caramel Sauce

•

With deviled eggs riding high on skewers set into iceberg lettuce bases, Salad-On-A-Skewer looks a little like a listing sail boat.

A platter of assorted cheeses and warm, crisp crackers, or thin slices of cocktail rye bread buttered and then toasted, complement the egg and crab of the salad nicely.

If a rice pudding can be elegant, Rum Rice Pudding with Rum Caramel Sauce fits the description.

SALAD-ON-A-SKEWER

King Crab and Deviled Egg make this devilishly good.

Ingredients	4 Portions	24 Portions
Iceberg lettuce	1 head	6 heads
Alaska King Crab	1 can (7½ oz.) or ½ lb. frozen	6 cans (7½ oz.) or 3 lb. frozen
Soy oil	½ cup	3 cups
Tarragon-flavored wine vinegar	¼ cup	1½ cups
Catsup or barbecue sauce	1 Tbsp.	¼ cup + 2 Tbsp.
Dried dill weed	⅛ tsp.	¾ tsp.
Salad seasoning	1 tsp.	2 Tbsp.
Salt	¼ tsp.	1½ Tbsp.
Chopped sweet pickle	2 Tbsp.	¾ cup
Chopped pimiento	1 Tbsp.	⅓ cup
Syrup from sweet pickles	1 tsp.	2 Tbsp.
Lemon slices	4 small	24 small
Lime slices	4 small	24 small
Hard-cooked *or* deviled egg halves	4	24

Core, rinse and thoroughly drain lettuce; chill in disposable plastic bag or plastic crisper. Drain crab. Select and set aside the larger pieces for the dressing (2 oz. and ¾ lb.)

Combine oil, vinegar, catsup, dill, salad seasoning, salt, pickle, pimiento and pickle syrup. Shake together in covered jar until well blended. Add remaining finely sliced crab.

Cut each head of lettuce lengthwise into 4 wedges; arrange on salad plates. For each portion arrange the large pieces of crab, an egg half, and lemon and lime slice on a skewer. Set skewers firmly into lettuce wedges or place alongside lettuce on salad plate. Serve with the crab dressing.

RUM RICE PUDDING

Everyone loves rice pudding, and it is doubly good served with Rum Caramel Sauce

Ingredients	4 Portions	24 Portions
Raisins	½ cup	3 cups
Rum	2 Tbsp.	¾ cup
Lemon juice and rind	1 tsp.	2 Tbsp.
Rice	¼ cup	1½ cups

Milk	2 cups	12 cups
Salt	¼ tsp.	1½ tsp.
Butter	2 Tbsp.	12 Tbsp.
Eggs, separated	2	12
Sugar	½ cup	3 cups
Nutmeg	¼ tsp.	1½ tsp.

To raisins add rum, lemon juice and rind. Let stand 2 hours or overnight.

Put rice, milk and salt in top of double boiler; cook for 1 hour, stirring often. Combine with butter, egg yolks, sugar and nutmeg. Cool.

Beat egg whites until stiff; fold in cold rice mixture.

Pour into greased casserole. Place casserole in pan of hot water. Bake at 325°F for 35 minutes.

RUM CARAMEL SAUCE

Can also be used as a dessert fondue or as a topping for cake or ice cream sprinkled with toasted almonds.

Ingredients	4 Portions	24 Portions
Sugar	¾ cup	4½ cups
Salt	To taste	To taste
Heavy cream, warmed	1 cup	1 quart + 1 pint
Dark rum	1 tsp.	2 Tbsp.
Vanilla extract	¼ tsp.	1½ tsp.

Melt sugar and salt in a heavy pan over low heat, stirring to prevent burning.

Remove pan from heat and slowly stir in warmed cream, rum and vanilla; stir together until smooth.

Keep warm over hot water until serving time.

Vichyssoise
Gherkin Beef Salad
Corn on the Cob
Swiss Peasant Bread
Blueberry Crunch Pie

•

An ideal menu to prepare ahead for a patio party; no one wants to do kitchen duty while guests are whooping it up and wolfing it down.

The Gherkin Beef Salad is a simple way to use any roast you want to prepare. But if you don't want to cook, you can use ready-cooked, or deli-counter beef, just as well. The dressing adds both moistness and piquancy.

Corn on the cob can be roasted on the grill, if you're dining outdoors, and the bread can also be heated on the grill.

Blueberry Crunch Pie is the real winner. There's no piecrust to fuss with. You just spread blueberries in a pie pan, top with the batter and bake. At serving time, you invert it and have an up-side-down pie to be served warm with ice cream or whipped cream. If you've done this a day ahead, just warm in a microwave or your regular oven while you're heating the bread.

GHERKIN BEEF SALAD

Almost any cold cooked beef can be used with vinaigrette.

VINAIGRETTE DRESSING

Ingredients	6 Portions	24 Portions
Wine vinegar	3 Tbsp.	¾ cup
Soy oil	¾ cup	3 cups
Salt	¼ tsp.	1 tsp.
Dry mustard	¼ tsp.	1 tsp.
Black pepper	⅛ tsp.	½ tsp.
Parsley, chopped	2 Tbsp.	½ cup
Tarragon leaves	1 tsp.	1 Tbsp. + 1 tsp.
Chives, chopped	1 Tbsp.	¼ cup
Chervil	1 tsp.	1 Tbsp. + 1 tsp.
Sweet pickle liquid	2 Tbsp.	½ cup
Sweet gherkins, sliced	½ cup	2 cups

Combine vinegar, oil, all seasonings, pickle liquid and some of the gherkins. Let stand at least 1 hour.

If meat has been refrigerated, allow to warm to room temperature or place on tray in 300°F oven for about 5 minutes to warm slightly.

SALAD

Ingredients	6 Portions	24 Portions
Beef, cooked (roast beef, pot roast or steak), cold, cut ¼ to ½ inch thick	6 slices	24 slices
Lettuce leaves		
Onion, thinly sliced, separated into rings	1	4
Tomatoes, cut in wedges	2	8

Arrange meat, lettuce leaves and onion rings in overlapping layers on large serving platter. Place tomato wedges around edge and sprinkle remaining gherkins over top.

Just before serving, spoon vinaigrette dressing over meat and vegetables. Serve remaining dressing in small bowl.

BLUEBERRY CRUNCH PIE

An upside-down dessert to serve warm with whipped cream
or ice cream.

Ingredients	6 Portions	24 Portions
Blueberries	3 cups	12 cups
Sugar	1¼ cups	5 cups
Walnuts, chopped	½ cup	2 cups
Flour	1 cup	4 cups
Butter or margarine	2 Tbsp.	½ cup
Eggs, beaten	2	8
Orange rind, grated	¼ tsp.	1 tsp.
Vanilla extract	¼ tsp.	1 tsp.
Nutmeg, grated	⅛ tsp.	½ tsp.
Cinnamon, ground	⅛ tsp.	½ tsp.

Preheat oven to 325°F.

Spread berries in well-buttered pie pan. Sprinkle with ¾ cup (3 cups) sugar and the nuts.

Beat together remaining sugar, flour, butter, eggs, grated orange rind, vanilla, nutmeg and cinnamon until smooth. Pour over berries. Bake 1 hour. Turn upside-down and serve warm.

Brandied Berry Soup
Salmon Sandwich
Avocado Dressing
Sliced Tomatoes with Fresh Tarragon
Heavenly Pie

•

Brandied Berry Soup can be prepared well ahead of the luncheon as it must be served chilled. The soup is made from pureed berries and brandy with more berries sliced and added at the last moment. Decorate each bowlful with a small spoonful of sour cream and a mint sprig or a thin strawberry slice.

The Avocado Dressing makes a pretty open-faced sandwich with the green of the dressing drizzled over the pink salmon.

Heavenly Pie is a recipe which a friend, Phyllis Hart, gave me years ago. It is a meringue with nuts and dates and simple as sin to make. Serve it with whipped cream, ice cream or frozen yogurt.

BRANDIED BERRY SOUP

Pink and pretty, strawberries and brandy, to serve on either end of the meal.

Ingredients	6 Portions	24 Portions
Fresh strawberries	5 cups	20 cups
Brandy	1½ cups	6 cups
Sugar	⅓ cup	1⅓ cups
Salt	⅛ tsp.	½ tsp.
Cornstarch	1 Tbsp.	4 Tbsp.
Red grape juice, bottled	2 cups	2 quarts
Lemon juice	2 tsp.	2 Tbsp. + 2 tsp.

Halve 4 cups (16 cups) berries and combine with 1 cup (4 cups) brandy, sugar and salt. Heat just to boiling. Turn into blender jar and puree; pour through fine wire strainer to remove seeds.

Blend cornstarch with remaining brandy. Stir into berry mixture; add red grape juice. Bring to boil, then cook and stir just until clear and slightly thickened. Remove from heat, stir in lemon juice, cover and chill.

When ready to serve, slice remaining berries and add to chilled soup.

Decorate with small spoonful of sour cream and a mint sprig, if desired.

SALMON SANDWICH with AVOCADO DRESSING

A whole meal in a hearty sandwich with a lot of eye appeal.

Ingredients	6 Portions	24 Portions
Salmon, canned or cooked	¾ lb.	3 lb.
Lemon juice	2 Tbsp.	½ cup
Celery, chopped	1 cup	4 cups
Bohemian rye bread slices	12	48
Butter, softened	As needed	As needed
Lettuce leaves	6	24
Tomato slices	12	48
Lettuce, shredded	1 cup	4 cups
Paprika	As needed	As needed

Drain salmon, skin, bone and flake. Add lemon juice and celery and refrigerate.

Lightly butter bread. Top one slice of bread with a lettuce leaf and 2 slices of tomato. Place shredded lettuce on other slice of bread and cover with salmon mixture.

Stripe with *Avocado Dressing* (recipe follows); sprinkle lightly with paprika. Serve open face.

Ingredients	6 Portions	24 Portions
Mayonnaise	1 cup	1 quart
Avocado, mashed	½ cup	2 cups
Sour cream	¼ cup	1 cup
Onion, minced	1 tsp.	1 Tbsp. + 1 tsp.
Salt	To taste	To taste
Tabasco	To taste	To taste

Combine all ingredients and blend thoroughly. Cover and refrigerate.

HEAVENLY PIE

Really a date-nut cake baked in pie form.

Ingredients	6 Portions (1 Pie)	24 Portions (4 Pies)
Eggs, separated	2	8
Brown sugar	¾ cup	3 cups
Nuts, chopped	1 cup	4 cups
Dates, chopped	1 cup	4 cups
All-purpose flour, sifted	3 Tbsp.	¾ cup
Baking powder	1 tsp.	1 Tbsp. + 1 tsp.
Salt	½ tsp.	2 tsp.
Rum flavoring, optional	½ tsp.	2 tsp.

Preheat oven to 300°F.

Beat egg yolks with brown sugar; stir in nuts and dates. Sift flour, baking powder and salt into batter and stir to combine.

Fold in flavoring and stiffly beaten egg whites. Bake 30 minutes or until done.

Serve with a rum sauce or whipped cream flavored with rum.

Show-Off Sandwich Shapes
Frosted Party Loaf
Super Sandwich Fillings
Orange Melba
Frosted Fruit Drinks
Tea Cookies

•

Fancy buffet luncheons can be no more trouble than you choose to make them.

With several fillings in different shapes, a little variety can be made to look like a lot of variation. Sandwich loaves are particularly impressive on a buffet, because they're frosted with a cream cheese mixture and decorated. They're even prettier on the inside if you alternate white and whole-grain breads as you stack and fill.

Orange Melba is a variation on the famous Peach Melba. Actually a raspberry Melba Sauce goes beautifully with any fruit, poached or raw, and vanilla ice cream.

SHOW-OFF SANDWICH SHAPES

PINWHEEL SANDWICHES

Remove crusts from unsliced loaf of bread. Slice loaf lengthwise into slices ¼-inch thick. Roll each slice with a rolling pin to flatten. Spread with your choice of fillings. Place stuffed olives, gherkins, or other small piece of vegetable across one of the short ends. Starting at end with olives, tightly roll up bread. Wrap rolls in waxed paper, foil or plastic wrap, twisting ends securely. Refrigerate several hours, or overnight. To serve, cut chilled rolls into thin slices; for more decorative slices spread outside of rolls with softened butter and roll in chopped parsley or chopped nuts before slicing.

OPEN-FACE SANDWICHES

Cut slices of bread with cookie cutter or with a knife into geometric shapes. Spread with sandwich filling. Garnish with sliced stuffed olives, gherkins, parsley sprigs, cucumber slices, strips of pimiento, carrot circles, sliced radishes, or slices of hard-cooked eggs.

SEE-THROUGH SANDWICHES

With cookie cutter, cut bread slices into rounds; with smaller cutter, cut hole in center of half of rounds. Spread whole rounds with sandwich filling; top with open circles. Place garnish in opening. Garnish with olive circles, carrot slices, gherkin fans, radish slices, cucumber pieces, pimiento strips or hard-cooked eggs.

LILY SANDWICHES

Trim crusts from slices of bread; roll gently with rolling pin to flatten. Spread sandwich filling on bread. With corner of bread facing you, fold left and right corners to middle to form a cone. Press gently to hold in place, or use a toothpick. Place sliver of olive, tomato or pickle in open end of sandwich to resemble the center of a lily. Roll in waxed paper, aluminum foil or plastic wrap. Refrigerate several hours or overnight.

FROSTED PARTY LOAF

You don't need to be an artist to decorate a loaf beautifully.

Ingredients	8 Portions	24 Portions
3 Sandwich Fillings, of your choice	1 cup each	3 cups each
Cucumber, sliced paper thin	1	3
White bread, unsliced	1 loaf	3 loaves
Butter or margarine, softened to room temperature	2 Tbsp.	¼ cup + 2 Tbsp.
Cream cheese, softened to room temperature	1 lb.	3 lb.
Parsley, chopped	⅓ cup	1 cup

Prepare fillings.

Place cucumber slices on paper towel to absorb excess moisture.

Cut all crusts from bread with sharp knife. Lay loaf on its side; cut into 5 even slices; spread first slice with soft butter, overlap cucumber slices.

Spread one slice each with 3 fillings. Stack slices; top with fifth slice of bread.

Beat cream cheese until smooth; spread on top and sides of loaf. Gently press chopped parsley on sides of loaf.

To make flower garnish on top, use strips of green pepper or cucumber skin for flower stems, and circles of carrots, radishes, black or green olives for flowers.

SUPER SANDWICH FILLINGS

SAVORY TUNA

Ingredients	6 Portions	24 Portions
Tuna, flaked	1 can (6½ or 7 oz.)	4 cans
Celery, chopped	¼ cup	1 cup
Mayonnaise	¼ cup	1 cup
Pickle relish	2 Tbsp.	½ cup
Capers, chopped	2 Tbsp.	½ cup

In medium bowl, combine all ingredients; mix well.

EGG SALAD

Ingredients	6 Portions	24 Portions
Eggs, hard-cooked, chopped	4	16
Celery, chopped	¼ cup	1 cup

Mayonnaise	2 Tbsp.	½ cup
Salt	¼ tsp.	1 tsp.
Pepper	To taste	To taste

In medium bowl, combine all ingredients; mix well.

TUNA APPLE CHEESE SPREAD

Particularly suited to open-face sandwiches.

Ingredients	*2 Cups*	*8 Cups*
Tuna, in oil or water	1 can (6½ or 7 oz.)	4 cans
Cream cheese, softened to room temperature	1 pkg. (3 oz.)	¾ lb.
Apple, unpeeled, chopped	1 small	4 small
Walnuts, chopped	¼ cup	1 cup
Parsley, chopped	2 Tbsp.	¾ cup
Milk	2 Tbsp.	¾ cup
Lemon juice	½ tsp.	2 tsp.
Nutmeg, ground	½ tsp.	2 tsp.

Drain excess liquid from tuna.

In medium bowl, break tuna into fine flakes. Add remaining ingredients; mix well.

TUNA LEMON BUTTER

A fine filling for lily sandwiches.

Ingredients	*1½ Cups*	*6 Cups*
Tuna, in oil or water	1 can (6½ or 7 oz.)	4 cans (6½ or 7 oz.)
Butter or margarine, softened to room temperature	6 Tbsp.	24 Tbsp. (3 sticks)
Celery, chopped	¼ cup	1 cup
Ripe olives, chopped	2 Tbsp.	½ cup
Fresh chives, chopped	1 Tbsp.	¼ cup
Lemon juice	2 tsp.	2 Tbsp. + 2 tsp.
Lemon rind, grated	1 tsp.	1 Tbsp. + 1 tsp.

Drain excess liquid from tuna.

In medium bowl, break tuna into fine flakes. Add remaining ingredients; mix well.

ORANGE MELBA

The raspberry Melba Sauce is equally delicious served with any fruit and ice cream.

Ingredients	6 Portions	24 Portions
Cornstarch	2 tsp.	2 Tbsp. + 2 tsp.
Water	⅓ cup	1⅓ cups
Frozen raspberries, thawed	1 pkg. (10 oz.)	4 pkg. (40 oz.)
Fresh grated lemon peel	½ tsp.	2 tsp.
Fresh squeezed lemon juice	1 Tbsp.	¼ cup
Navel oranges, peeled, chilled	2 large or 3 medium	8 large or 12 medium
Vanilla ice cream	1½ pints	3 quarts

In a small saucepan mix cornstarch and water. Add thawed raspberries, lemon peel and juice. Cook over medium heat until clear and slightly thickened, about 2 to 3 minutes. Remove from heat and cool.

Slice chilled oranges into cartwheels. Cut each cartwheel slice into quarters. Arrange quarter cartwheels in six individual serving dishes.

Top with scoops of vanilla ice cream. Pour Melba sauce over ice cream and serve.

Lima Minestrone
Italiano Sandwich
Tossed Green Salad with Italian Dressing
Chocolate Peppermint Torte

•

Lima Minestrone is a hale and hearty soup and the open-faced Italiano sandwich is equally robust. In addition to Italian sausage, the Italian bread holds ground beef, ricotta cheese and Mozzarella cheese which melts over all when the sandwich is broiled—hearty, indeed.

A green salad adds a light touch and though the Chocolate Peppermint Torte is sinfully rich, no one ever virtuously turns it down.

LIMA MINESTRONE

Very quick and easy with fresh or frozen vegetables.

Ingredients	6 Portions	24 Portions
Onion, chopped	½ cup	2 cups
Butter or margarine	1 Tbsp.	4 Tbsp.
Chicken broth	1 quart + 1 cup	1 gallon + 1 quart
Salt	To taste	To taste
Italian herb seasoning	½ tsp.	2 tsp.
Basil, crumbled	¼ tsp.	1 tsp.
Spinach, frozen, chopped	1 pkg. (10 oz.)	4 pkg. (2½ lb.)
or	or	or
Spinach, fresh, chopped	3 cups	12 cups
Baby lima beans, frozen	1 pkg. (10 oz.)	4 pkg. (2½ lb.)
or	or	or
Baby lima beans, fresh	1½ cups	6 cups
Salad macaroni, uncooked	¼ cup	1 cup
Tomatoes, canned	1 can (1 lb.)	4 cans (4 lb.)

Saute onion lightly in butter. Add broth, salt, Italian herb seasoning and basil. Heat to boiling.

Add spinach and limas, and heat until vegetables can be broken up. Add macaroni and simmer 10 minutes.

Add tomatoes, breaking up larger pieces, and heat through.

ITALIANO SANDWICH

A knife-and-fork sandwich.

Ingredients	6 Sandwiches	24 Sandwiches
Italian sausage, natural casing, hot	1 lb.	4 lb.
Beef, ground	½ lb.	2 lb.
Spaghetti sauce	1 jar (15 oz.)	4 jars (60 oz.)
Italian bread	12 slices	48 slices
Ricotta cheese	1½ cups (12 oz.)	6 cups (3 lb.)
Green olives, stuffed and chopped	½ cup	2 cups
Mushrooms, sliced and drained	1 can (4 oz.)	4 cans (1 lb.)
Mozzarella cheese	12 slices	48 slices

Brown sausage and beef; drain. Stir in spaghetti sauce and keep warm.

Spread each bread slice with Ricotta cheese. Spoon meat sauce over top. Sprinkle with olives and mushrooms.

Top with cheese slices. Broil about 6 inches from heat until cheese melts, 3 to 5 minutes. Serve open-faced.

CHOCOLATE PEPPERMINT TORTE

It's a rich dessert, but "worth the calories."

Ingredients	1 Torte	2 Tortes
Butter or margarine, soft	½ cup	1 cup
Sugar	¾ cup	1½ cups
Chocolate, unsweetened and melted	3 oz.	6 oz.
Vanilla	1 tsp.	2 tsp.
Peppermint flavoring	¾ tsp.	1½ tsp.
Eggs	3	6
Cream, heavy and whipped	½ cup	1 cup
Chocolate, grated unsweetened or chocolate curls		

Prepare crust (recipe follows) and set aside.

In a mixer bowl beat butter until creamy; gradually add sugar and beat until light and fluffy, then beat in chocolate, vanilla, and peppermint flavoring.

Add eggs, one at a time, beating for 3 minutes after each addition. Fold in the whipped cream, then spoon into the crumb crust. Sprinkle generously with grated chocolate.

Cover lightly and chill at least 4 hours or overnight. Remove rim before serving.

CHOCOLATE CRUMB CRUST

Ingredients	1 Crust	2 Crusts
Chocolate wafer crumbs	1 cup	2 cups
Butter, melted	2 Tbsp.	4 Tbsp.

Preheat oven to 350°F.

Stir ingredients together. Lightly press into the bottom of a 9-inch cake pan with a removable bottom.

Bake for 7 minutes or until toasted. Cool.

Chilled Artichokes
Fresh Lemon Dressing
Toasted Sandwich Loaf
Olives, Pickles, Cherry Tomatoes
Pineapple Cheesecake Tortoni

•

This entire menu can be prepared ahead, freeing the hostess, or host, to enjoy the guests.

Half an artichoke per person is really enough to satisfy most appetites, particularly at lunch. The artichokes are cooked and chilled—then cut in half lengthwise. The Fresh Lemon Dressing should be served so that each guest has a small dipping bowl for his own use. Small Japanese rice bowls are perfect.

Toasted Sandwich Loaf looks very special but is made simply by stacking sandwiches together upright with a skewer to keep them from slipping. Assemble it well ahead, and then warm it for 30 minutes—to melt the cheese and heat the bread—immediately before serving.

You can buy macaroons and crumble them as an ingredient in Pineapple Cheesecake Tortoni, or you can make your own. Either way, the finished dessert is elegant, layered in pretty glasses and frozen firm.

CHILLED ARTICHOKES with FRESH LEMON DRESSING

Serve as an appetizer, a vegetable or a salad.

Ingredients	6 Portions	24 Portions
Artichokes	3	12
Salt	1½ tsp.	2 Tbsp.
Carrots, quartered	2	8
Onion, small	1	4

Rinse artichokes in cold water. Turn each on its side. With a sharp knife cut off about 1 inch from top. Cut off stem close to base. Pull off coarse leaves around bottom. Snip off sharp leaf tips with scissors.

In a large kettle or saucepan bring 3 inches of water to a boil. Add salt and artichokes, and place carrots and onion between artichokes. Cover and simmer 30 to 35 minutes or until artichoke base is fork tender and a leaf pulls easily from base. Drain upside down and chill. (The cooking liquid has very good flavor. Save to use in stews or soups.)

Before serving, split lengthwise, remove and discard chokes. Serve artichoke halves with *Fresh Lemon Dressing* (recipe follows).

FRESH LEMON DRESSING

Enhances any salad or vegetable.

Ingredients	6 Portions	24 Portions
Fresh lemon juice	3 Tbsp.	¾ cup
Salad oil	6 Tbsp.	1½ cups
Salt	½ tsp.	2 tsp.
Pepper	¼ tsp.	1 tsp.
Dry mustard	¼ tsp.	1 tsp.
Parsley, chopped	2 Tbsp.	½ cup
Garlic clove, halved	1	4

Mix all ingredients in small bowl.

Let stand at room temperature about 1 hour. Remove garlic before serving.

TOASTED SANDWICH LOAF

Sandwiches baked on a skewer.

Ingredients	8 Portions (1 Loaf)	24 Portions (3 Loaves)
Whole grain bread, 1 lb. loaves	1	3
Ham, thinly sliced	16 slices	48 slices

Swiss or sharp cheddar cheese, sliced	8 oz.	1½ lb.
Sharp mustard	To taste	To taste
Alfalfa sprouts	2 cups	6 cups
Butter, melted	½ cup	1½ cups
Garlic, minced	½ tsp.	1½ tsp.
Parmesan cheese, grated	2 Tbsp.	¼ cup + 2 Tbsp.

Preheat oven to 350°F.

Make sandwiches using 2 bread slices, spreading 1 side of each slice of bread with mustard. Place 2 ham slices, 1 slice of cheese and ¼ cup of sprouts between bread. Spear sandwiches together in the shape of the original loaf using heat-proof skewers. Place on shallow, foil-lined pan.

Combine remaining ingredients and spoon over loaf. Open slices to allow butter mixture to run into loaf.

Bake 30 to 35 minutes. Pull sandwiches apart and serve piping hot.

PINEAPPLE CHEESECAKE TORTONI

Pineapple layered with a rum-cheese-cream combination, then topped with macaroon crumbs and frozen.

Ingredients	6 Portions	30 Portions
Pineapple, canned coarse crushed, in juice, drained	10 oz. (1 cup + 3 Tbsp.)	3 lb. (1½ quarts)
Sugar	⅓ cup	1⅔ cups
Juice from pineapple	1½ Tbsp.	½ cup
Cherries, candied, coarsely cut	2 Tbsp.	½ cup + 2 Tbsp.
Cream cheese	1 pkg. (3 oz.)	1 lb.
Light rum	1 Tbsp. (½ oz.)	5 Tbsp. (3 oz.)
Heavy cream	¾ cup	1 quart
Confectioners' sugar, sifted	¼ cup	1¼ cups
Vanilla	½ tsp.	1 Tbsp.
Salt	Pinch	¼ tsp.
Macaroon crumbs	½ cup	2½ cups

Combine pineapple, sugar and juice from pineapple. Boil together, until thick, stirring occasionally. Cool, then stir in cherries.

Soften cream cheese. Beat in rum, mixing until smooth.

Beat cream with confectioners' sugar, vanilla and salt to soft peaks. Fold in cheese mixture.

In individual serving glasses, place a scoop pineapple mixture. Top with scoop cheese cream. Sprinkle with 1 Tbsp. macaroon crumbs.

Repeat pineapple and cheese layers as before. Top with 1 tsp. pineapple, and light sprinkling of crumbs.

Freeze until firm.

Crab Salad with Caper Mayonnaise
Warm Colonial Bread
Rhubarb Cream Pie

•

We tend to think of crab as being a budget breaker, but when you consider that there is absolutely no waste, and you don't have to give each guest an entire crab, it proves not to be as expensive as your guests will think it is.

Caper Mayonnaise helps bring out the full crab flavor and warm Colonial Bread—a rye, whole grain, and wheat germ bread—complements the salad.

Rhubarb Cream Pie is a lovely, light, very American way to fill any spaces left.

CRAB SALAD

The orange and green of the avocado and orange slices make this a very pretty salad, and the Caper Mayonnaise accents both the fruit and the crab. It can also be served with egg or other accouterments.

Ingredients	4 Portions	24 Portions
Iceberg lettuce	1 head	6 heads
Avocado	1 small	6 small
Orange	1 large	6 large
Alaska King crab	1 can (7½ oz.) or ½ lb. frozen	6 cans (7½ oz.) or 3 lb. frozen

Core, rinse and drain lettuce thoroughly; chill until crisp in disposable plastic bag or plastic crisper. Cut avocado in half, remove seed and skin; cut fruit into crosswise slices. Pare orange; cut into slices, then cut each slice in half.

With sharp knife, cut lettuce crosswise into 4 slices or "rafts" about ¾ inch thick. Refrigerate remaining lettuce to use another time.

Arrange lettuce rafts on individual salad plates. Starting from the outside, arrange overlapping slices of avocado in a circle, then orange slices. Pile drained, sliced crabmeat in center. Top with Caper Mayonnaise (recipe follows).

CAPER MAYONNAISE

Ingredients	¾ Cup	4½ Cups
Mayonnaise	⅔ cup	4 cups
Chili sauce	2 Tbsp.	¾ cup
Capers	1½ tsp.	3 Tbsp.
Seasoned salt	¼ tsp.	1½ tsp.
Prepared mustard	¼ tsp.	1½ tsp.
Lemon juice	1 tsp.	2 Tbsp.

Blend all ingredients together. Cover and chill.

COLONIAL BREAD

There are four different grains in this hearty bread.

Ingredients	2 Loaves	6 Loaves
Yellow corn meal	½ cup	1½ cups
Brown sugar	¼ cup	¾ cup
Salt	1 Tbsp.	3 Tbsp.

	2 cups	6 cups
Boiling water	2 cups	6 cups
Cooking oil	¼ cup	¾ cup
Dry yeast	2 pkg.	6 pkg.
Lukewarm water	½ cup	1½ cups
Whole wheat flour	¾ cup	2¼ cups
Rye flour	½ cup	1½ cups
Wheat germ	¼ cup	¾ cup
Flour, all-purpose	5 cups	15 cups

Combine corn meal, brown sugar, salt, oil, and boiling water. Cool to lukewarm. Soften yeast in lukewarm water and add to cooled corn meal mixture. Add whole wheat, rye flour and wheat germ. Add remaining flour to make a moderately stiff dough. Knead 6 to 8 minutes. Place in greased bowl. Let rise in warm place until double, 50 to 60 minutes.

Punch down; let rest 10 minutes. Shape into loaves and place in 9x5x3-inch greased loaf pans. Let rise until double.

Bake at 375°F for 45 minutes, or until done.

RHUBARB CREAM PIE

We don't often find rhubarb pie with a meringue; this one is a favorite in North Dakota.

Ingredients	1 Pie	4 Pies
Butter or margarine	2 Tbsp.	8 Tbsp. (1 stick)
Rhubarb, diced	2 cups	2 quarts
Sugar	1¼ cups	5 cups
Cornstarch	2 Tbsp.	½ cup
Light cream or half-and-half	¼ cup	1 cup
Egg yolks	3	12
Grated orange rind	¼ tsp.	1 tsp.
Salt	⅛ tsp.	½ tsp.

MERINGUE

Ingredients	1 Pie	4 Pies
Egg whites	3	12
Sugar	⅓ cup	1⅓ cups
Pie shell, baked 8-inch	1	4

Preheat oven to 350°F. In a saucepan, melt butter, then add rhubarb and sugar; cook slowly until rhubarb is tender. Combine cornstarch with cream and egg yolks; stir into rhubarb mixture, then add orange rind and salt. Cook together until thick.

Pour into baked pie shell and top with meringue made by beating egg whites together with sugar until almost like divinity candy. Bake 12 to 15 minutes, until nicely browned.

Japanese Cocktail Crackers
Egg Drop Soup
Sake Beef Sandwiches
Nectarine Halves filled with Blueberries
Tea

•

Japanese cocktail crackers come in many varieties, all of them delicious with soup and salads.

This soup is an Americanized version of one the Japanese make by flavoring water with kelp and dried, flaked bonito (fish). If you wish you can substitute 3 cups of water for the chicken broth and bring to a boil with a 3-inch strip of washed kelp. Remove the kelp immediately or it will make the broth too strong. Add a few flakes (about half an ounce) of dried bonito when the kelp is removed. When the bonito has settled to the bottom pour off the broth and proceed as directed.

Sake Beef is made with cellophane noodles and eaten by wrapping the mixture in lettuce leaves and eating with your fingers.

Any kind of fruit in season would be a suitable dessert.

EGG DROP SOUP

The egg shreds and looks a little like chrysanthemum petals
in the soup.

Ingredients	6 Portions	24 Portions
Chicken broth	3 cups	3 quarts
Cornstarch	1 Tbsp.	¼ cup
Egg, well beaten	1	4
Green onion, sliced	2 Tbsp.	½ cup
Soy sauce	½ tsp.	2 tsp.

In saucepan slowly stir the chicken broth into cornstarch. Cook, stirring constantly, till slightly thickened. Slowly pour in the well-beaten egg; stir once gently. Remove from heat.

Garnish with green onion. Soy sauce may be added for seasoning at the table.

SAKE BEEF SANDWICHES

A most unusual sandwich with lettuce replacing bread.

Ingredients	6 Portions	24 Portions
Flank steak, sliced across grain, ½ inch thick	1 (1½ to 2 lb.)	4 (6 to 8 lb.)
Sake	2 Tbsp.	½ cup
Soy sauce	2 Tbsp.	½ cup
Garlic, crushed	1 clove	4 cloves
Ginger root	2 pieces	8 pieces
Soy oil	as needed	as needed
Cellophane noodles	1 8-oz. package	4 8-oz. packages
Cornstarch	2 Tbsp.	½ cup
Salt	1 tsp.	1 Tbsp. + 1 tsp.
Scallions, chopped	2	8
Lettuce	1 head	4 heads

Slice beef into ½-inch strips. Marinate in sake, soy sauce, garlic and ginger root. Heat some of the oil in large saucepan. Drop in noodles, cook for a few seconds until they "pop" up and expand. Place them on a large plate.

Heat remaining oil in a wok and add drained beef. Stir-fry, cooking quickly and stirring constantly until beef is cooked.

To the marinade add salt and cornstarch, stir to a smooth paste. Pour over the beef and stir over medium heat until thickened; add scallions. Pour over the noodles.

Core lettuce; wash and separate leaves; drain. To eat, use lettuce leaves and wrap filling as a sandwich.

TEA SANDWICHES AND PARTY LOAF
(courtesy of Tuna Research Foundation)

AVOCADO CHEF'S SALAD
(courtesy of California Avocado Commission)

TUNA BRIOCHE RING
(courtesy of Tuna Research Foundation)

GHERKIN BEEF SALAD
(courtesy of Pickle Packers International, Inc.)

WALNUT BRUNCH BREADS
(courtesy of Diamond Walnut Growers, Stockton, California)

SERVING SUGGESTIONS FOR CRAB SALAD
(courtesy of California Iceberg Lettuce Commission)

LOBSTER POTATO SALAD
(courtesy of South African Rock Lobster Service Corporation)

CORNISH HENS VALENCIENNE
(courtesy of Uncle Ben's Foods)

FLANK STEAK TERIYAKI AND JAPANESE VEGETABLES
(courtesy of Minute® Rice)

PINEAPPLE CHEESECAKE TORTONI
(courtesy of Pineapple Growers' Association of Hawaii)

INDIAN CHICKEN KORMA AND DAHL SOUP
(courtesy of American Spice Trade Association)

LETTUCE SOUFFLÉ
(courtesy of California Iceberg Lettuce Commission)

TWO

The Elegant Egg

The simple egg is probably the most versatile source of protein we have and certainly the least expensive. From it come light and lovely soufflés, puffy or flat omelets, crepes of all descriptions, quiche, baked eggs, poached eggs, soft and hard-cooked eggs, scrambled and fried eggs. The egg can be used as a binding agent or an extender.

Omelets, soufflés and crepes may seem to be frightening, but they only take a little practice. When making crepes (and do make and freeze them in quantity) prepare the batter as much as 24 hours ahead; the crepes will not tear as readily and will be easier to flip. Also, be certain you have a well-seasoned pan.

The secret with omelets is to heat the pan thoroughly before adding the eggs. Don't add the fat or the omelet mixture until the pan's heat will make ½ teaspoon of water separate into beads like mercury. Again, have a well-seasoned pan, so that the omelet slides freely once set. Omelets can be made as much as 25 minutes before serving.

Soufflés, on the other hand, depend upon lightness for their appeal. Always be certain that your beaters or wire whip are entirely fat free. Whenever possible beat the egg whites first and then the yolks, or use two separate sets of beaters. Some recipes will call for cream of tartar to help the whites stand up a few minutes longer. Soufflés wilt fast—they really must be served almost immediately.

I personally feel that all soufflés deserve a sauce. When making a dessert soufflé, I hold back a bit of the batter and combine it with softened ice cream and a liqueur to make a lovely, light sauce. When serving a vegetable or seafood soufflé nothing could be more flattering than Hollandaise Sauce.

Never, never boil an egg—it toughens the protein. The proper cooking temperature is just under boiling; cool the eggs quickly if you want to peel them without tearing the whites. Older eggs will peel a bit more easily than fresh ones.

You can judge an egg's freshness by how high the yolk stands when the egg is broken: the higher the yolk, the fresher the egg. Use only the freshest eggs for egg entrees, the less fresh for baking. When you are hard-cooking them, use a small pin to pierce the broad end before putting the egg in water; it won't crack while cooking.

Pecans Toasted with Garlic Salt
Scotch Eggs
Banana Waffles
Apricot Banana Sauce

•

Sprinkle pecans with garlic salt and place in the toaster oven to warm while preparing the Scotch Eggs.

The eggs make a remarkably impressive dish—hard-cooked eggs coated with a ham mixture, then rolled in bread crumbs and deep fried. The secret is to have the fat at 375°F before adding the eggs (a few at a time to keep the temperature up).

The sweetness of Apricot Banana Sauce goes well with the ham and the Banana Waffles serve as a starch, a bread, and a dessert—three for the work of one. Frozen waffles could be used, but the banana flavor is a welcome change.

SCOTCH EGGS

Hard-cooked eggs are coated with ham, then deep fried until golden brown.

Ingredients	8 Portions	24 Portions
Ground cooked ham	2 cups (about ½ lb.)	6 cups (about 1½ lb.)
Raw eggs	2	6
Dried leaf thyme	½ tsp.	1½ tsp.
Tabasco sauce	¼ tsp.	¾ tsp.
Prepared mustard	1 tsp.	1 Tbsp.
Hard-cooked eggs, peeled	8	24
Fine dry bread crumbs	1½ cups	4½ cups
Soy oil for frying		

In bowl mix ham, raw eggs, thyme, Tabasco and mustard. Pat ham mixture around hard-cooked eggs to make even coating; roll in bread crumbs. Heat oil for deep frying in heavy saucepan or deep fryer to 375°F. Add coated eggs, a few at a time, and fry until golden brown, 2 or 3 minutes.

Drain on paper towels. Serve warm or cold.

BANANA WAFFLES

A "different" desert, lunch or brunch dish.

Ingredients	8 Portions	24 Portions
Unsifted all-purpose flour	4 cups	12 cups
Baking powder	2 Tbsp.	¼ cup + 2 Tbsp.
Salt	½ tsp.	1½ tsp.
Grated lemon peel, optional	1 tsp.	1 Tbsp.
Eggs, separated	6	18
Milk	2½ cups	7½ cups
Butter or margarine, melted	6 Tbsp.	18 Tbsp.
Ripe bananas, mashed	2 cups (6 medium)	6 cups (18 medium)

In large bowl mix flour, baking powder, salt and lemon peel.

In another bowl beat together egg yolks, milk, melted butter and mashed bananas. Add all at once to dry mixture; stir just enough to moisten.

Beat egg whites until stiff but not dry; fold into batter. Let batter stand for 5 to 10 minutes to develop banana flavor.

Bake in waffle iron according to manufacturer's directions.

Serve with Apricot Banana Sauce (recipe follows) or with sliced bananas and syrup.

APRICOT BANANA SAUCE

Waffles, French toast and pancakes all taste better with this fruit sauce—so does vanilla ice cream.

Ingredients	8 portions	24 Portions
Cornstarch	2 Tbsp.	6 Tbsp.
Salt	½ tsp.	1½ tsp.
Apricot nectar	3 cups	9 cups
Honey	6 Tbsp.	1 cup + 2 Tbsp.
Lemon juice	2 Tbsp.	6 Tbsp.
Butter or margarine	4 Tbsp.	12 Tbsp.
Bananas	4	12

In medium saucepan mix cornstarch and salt with a small amount of apricot nectar. Gradually stir in remaining apricot nectar and honey.

Cook over low heat, stirring constantly, until mixture thickens and comes to a boil. Remove from heat; add lemon juice and butter.

Peel bananas, slice and add to sauce.

Tuna Pine Cones
Lettuce Soufflé
Stuffed Tomato Salad
Swedish Apple Meringue Dessert

•

Tuna Pine Cones are appetizers so handsome that they can garnish other, plainer dishes. They are served on toast, melba rounds, or crackers, and can be enjoyed with the soufflé if you don't wish to serve them as a separate appetizer course.

The Lettuce Soufflé is an attention-getter which can be used as an appetizer at a dinner party. For appetizer use, make it in small soufflé cups.

This dessert is a little like a pie, but is baked square. The crust is tender, contains almonds and crumbles easily, giving texture to the filling and meringue. The apples for the filling are poached and then arranged over the crust which has been spread with raspberry jam.

TUNA PINE CONES

Fancy but easy.

Ingredients	4 Portions (8 Cones)	24 Portions (48 cones)
Tuna, drained and flaked	½ can (7 oz.)	3 cans (7 oz. ea.)
Ripe avocado, mashed	¼	1½
Butter or margarine	2 Tbsp.	¾ cup
Lemon juice	2 tsp.	4 Tbsp.
Pimiento, chopped	¼ tsp.	1½ tsp.
Onion, minced	1 tsp.	2 Tbsp.
Salt	Pinch	¼ tsp.
Tabasco sauce	Dash	¼ tsp.
Almonds, sliced, toasted	2 Tbsp.	¾ cup

In medium bowl, combine all ingredients except almonds; mix well. On waxed paper, divide mixture into 1 Tbsp. portions. Shape each portion into a pine cone.

Press almonds into tuna mixture to resemble "petals" of a pine cone.

To serve, place cones on crackers or melba rounds.

NOTE: To toast almonds, spread slices on cookie sheet and bake in 350°F oven 10 to 15 minutes or until lightly browned.

LETTUCE SOUFFLÉ

Flecks of green make this unusually attractive.

Ingredients	2 Portions	24 Portions
Iceberg lettuce, finely chopped	8 oz. (1 quart)	12 quarts
Butter or margarine	¼ cup	3 cups
Flour	3 Tbsp.	2¼ cups
Onion salt	½ tsp.	2 Tbsp.
Salt	½ tsp.	2 Tbsp.
Pepper	⅛ tsp.	1½ tsp.
Half-and-half or milk, scalded	1 cup	3 quarts
Worcestershire sauce	1 tsp.	¼ cup
Cheddar cheese, shredded	1 cup	12 cups
Eggs, separated	4	48
Cream of tartar	¼ tsp.	1 Tbsp.
Salt	Pinch	Pinch
Parmesan cheese, grated	¼ cup	3 cups

Cook lettuce, covered, in very little water until tender. Add 1 Tbsp. (¾ cup) butter; cook and stir until dry.

Melt remaining butter; blend in flour, onion salt, salt and pepper. Cook over low heat 3 to 5 minutes. Blend into half-and-half, along with Worcestershire; cook and stir until thickened. Remove from heat.

Add cheddar cheese; stir until melted. Beat in egg yolks, one at a time. Add cooked lettuce. (Preparation to this stage may be done ahead, mixture refrigerated and rewarmed—lukewarm, not hot—and completed as follows.)

Preheat oven to 400°F.

Beat egg whites (if desired, add one extra egg white) at low speed until foamy; add cream of tartar and pinch of salt and whip at high speed until stiff but not dry. Stir about ¼ into lettuce mixture; fold in remainder.

Pour into 6-cup mold(s) which has (have) been heavily buttered and coated with half the Parmesan. Tap on counter; smooth top. Sprinkle with remaining Parmesan.

Place in middle of oven. Reduce heat to 375°F. Bake 25 to 30 minutes. Turn off heat, but do not open oven door for at least 20 minutes.

SWEDISH APPLE MERINGUE DESSERT

The hint of raspberry makes it haunting.

Ingredients	6 Portions (1 Pie)	24 Portions (4 Pies)
CRUST		
Butter or margarine	⅓ cup	1⅓ cups
Sugar	3 Tbsp.	¾ cup
Egg yolks	2	8
All-purpose flour, sifted	¾ cup	3 cups
Almonds, roasted, chopped	⅓ cup	1⅓ cups
Lemon peel, grated	1 Tbsp.	¼ cup
Lemon juice	1 Tbsp.	¼ cup
FILLING		
Apples	4 to 6 medium	20 medium
Sugar	⅓ cup	1⅓ cups
Lemon juice	1½ Tbsp.	⅓ cup
Raspberry jam	½ cup	2 cups
MERINGUE		
Egg whites	2	8
Salt	Pinch	⅛ tsp.
Sugar	¼ cup	1 cup

Preheat oven to 350°F.

Cream butter; add sugar while continuing to cream. Add egg yolks; mix well. Add flour, almonds, lemon peel and lemon juice; blend well.

Press on bottom and sides of 9-inch pie pan(s). Brush with a little unbeaten egg white. Bake for 15 minutes, or until golden brown.

Pare and core apples; cut in eighths; combine with sugar and lemon juice in a saucepan; cover; cook over medium heat until tender.

Spread jam evenly over baked crust; arrange apples on top.

Beat egg whites with salt until stiff but not dry; add sugar, 1 Tbsp. at a time, while continuing to beat. Mound over apples.

Return to oven at 350°F for about 18 minutes or until meringue is lightly browned.

Danish Cucumbers
Reuben Omelet
Toasted Rye Bread
German Cream Cheese Brownies

•

Danish Cucumbers are delightful to have on hand summer or winter as they make an excellent appetizer, salad or even sandwich filling!

The Reuben Omelet combines the ingredients of the famous Reuben sandwich in omelet form. The recipe is for four servings, but you can have the ingredients ready, including the basic omelet mixture, and quickly make omelets to order. Guests are always impressed if you keep two pans (four servings) going at once.

Serve German Cream Cheese Brownies with ice cream and perhaps a hot fudge sauce.

DANISH CUCUMBERS

They keep almost indefinitely and you can replenish the supply once or twice by adding more sliced cucumbers and onion.

Ingredients	4 to 6 Portions	24 Portions
Cucumbers, sliced paper thin	1 large	5 large
Sweet onion, sliced paper thin	1 large	5 large
Dill, fresh, chopped	1 Tbsp.	1/3 cup
Tarragon vinegar	1/3 cup	2 cups
Sugar	3 Tbsp.	1 cup + 2 Tbsp.
Salt	1 tsp.	2 Tbsp.

Layer cucumber and onion slices in a container and sprinkle each layer with dill.

Combine remaining ingredients and pour over vegetables. The dressing will not cover the vegetables at first, but press down occasionally and it soon will. Marinate at least overnight.

REUBEN OMELET

The flavors match those of the Reuben sandwich and the omelet is almost as simple to prepare.

Ingredients	4 Portions	24 Portions
Corned beef, torn into bite-size pieces	8 slices	48 slices
Sauerkraut, well-drained	2/3 cup	4 cups
Caraway seeds	1/2 tsp.	1 Tbsp.
Swiss cheese, cut in strips	4 slices	24 slices
BASIC OMELET		
Eggs, beaten	4	24
Water	4 tsp.	1/2 cup
Salt	1/4 tsp.	1 1/2 tsp.
Tabasco sauce	1/8 tsp.	1 tsp.
Butter or margarine	2 Tbsp.	3/4 cup

In a medium bowl beat eggs, water, salt and Tabasco.

In 8½-inch omelet skillet(s) melt 1 Tbsp. butter over low heat; increase heat to moderately high. Pour half of egg mixture into pan and stir briskly with flat side of fork until almost set. Allow eggs to set and to brown lightly on bottom.

While top is still moist and creamy-looking, top with corned beef, sauerkraut, caraway seeds and Swiss cheese; slip under broiler to melt cheese.

With pancake turner, fold in half or roll, turning out onto platter with a quick flip of the wrist.

NOTE: Additional tips on omelet preparation are under recipe for *Avocado Omelet* and in the introduction to this chapter (see Index).

GERMAN CREAM CHEESE BROWNIES

The blend of rich chocolate and velvety cream cheese make these brownies special.

Ingredients	20 Brownies	40 Brownies
German sweet chocolate	1 pkg. (4 oz.)	2 pkg. (4 oz. ea.)
Butter	5 Tbsp.	½ cup + 2 Tbsp.
Cream cheese	1 pkg. (3 oz.)	2 pkg. (3 oz. ea.)
Sugar	1 cup	2 cups
Eggs	3	6
Flour, unsifted	½ cup + 1 Tbsp.	1 cup + 2 Tbsp.
Vanilla	1½ tsp.	1 Tbsp.
Baking powder	½ tsp.	1 tsp.
Salt	¼ tsp.	½ tsp.
Nuts, coarsely chopped	½ cup	1 cup
Almond extract	¼ tsp.	½ tsp.

Preheat oven to 350°F.

Melt chocolate and half of butter over very low heat, stirring constantly. Cool.

Cream remaining butter with the cream cheese until softened. Gradually add one-quarter of the sugar, creaming until light and fluffy. Stir in 1 (2) egg(s), 1 (2) Tbsp. flour, and ½ (1) tsp. vanilla until blended.

Beat remaining eggs until fluffy and light in color. Gradually add remaining sugar, beating until thickened. Fold in baking powder, salt and remaining flour. Blend in cooled chocolate mixture. Stir in nuts, almond extract, and remaining vanilla.

Measure 1 (2) cup(s) chocolate batter and set aside. Spread remaining chocolate batter in a greased 9-inch square pan (2 pans). Pour cheese mixture over the top. Drop reserved chocolate batter from tablespoon onto the cheese mixture; swirl the mixtures together with a spatula just to marble.

Bake 35 to 40 minutes. Cool. Cut in bars or squares. Cover and store in the refrigerator.

Blueberry Frappé
Brioche with Baked Eggs
Stir-Fry Spinach, Tomato and Bacon
Sliced Fresh Pineapple

•

Blueberry Frappé, made from fresh or frozen berries blended with any orange-flavored liqueur, Cassis (the French liqueur made from currants), or with orange juice, makes a most attractive appetizer. Serve it in wine glasses with a few berries and a sprig of mint for garnish.

While guests are sipping, you can be stir-frying the Spinach, Tomato and Bacon—cook the bacon ahead and have the vegetables chopped and ready to go.

The eggs can be baking in their brioche nest while you work. Either buy individual brioche, or bake a brioche ring, then hollow out little nests for the eggs to bake in. A brioche ring can be baked in any ring mold, or you can bake a large brioche in a fluted mold and cut off the bottom 3 inches to use for baking the eggs—keep the rest to serve as a bread at another meal.

BLUEBERRY FRAPPÉ

Serve as a cold soup, a beverage or as a dessert.

Ingredients	6 Portions	24 Portions
Half-and-half	1 pint	2 quarts
Blueberries, fresh or frozen	1 pint	2 quarts
Honey	¼ cup	1 cup
Any orange-flavored liqueur, Cassis, or orange juice	3 Tbsp.	¾ cup
Ice cubes	18	72
Fresh mint or blueberries	18	72

Place one half of blueberries, half-and-half, honey, liqueur in blender; whirl.

Gradually add ice to produce desired consistency. Repeat with second half.

Pour into chilled wine glasses and garnish with either mint sprigs or whole blueberries.

BRIOCHE with BAKED EGGS

This recipe can be made using individual brioche hollowed out to hold baked eggs, or with a brioche ring which you can make in a ring mold.

Ingredients	6 Portions	24 Portions
Brioche ring (recipe follows)		
Butter	¼ cup	1 cup
Eggs	6	24
Salt	To taste	To taste
Pepper	To taste	To taste
Heavy cream	⅔ cup	2⅔ cups

Preheat oven to 325°F.

Cut a thin slice from the top of a brioche. Hollow out 6 holes in the brioche at regular intervals, without cutting through the bottom crust.

Melt butter over low heat. Sprinkle the whole brioche with it, moistening the hollows well. Heat through in oven for 5 minutes. Remove brioche from oven.

Break an egg into each hollow and season. Return to oven for 5 minutes. Remove brioche once more. Pour the cream carefully over the top, surrounding each egg with it.

Return to oven for 5 minutes, or until eggs are set but yolks are still soft. Serve immediately.

BRIOCHE

Rich egg bread that keeps extremely well.

Ingredients	1 Large or 1 Dozen Small	4 Large or 4 Dozen Small
Milk	1 cup	1 quart
Butter	½ cup + 2 Tbsp.	2½ cups
Salt	1 tsp.	1 Tbsp. + 1 tsp.
Sugar	½ cup	2 cups
Dry yeast	2 pkg.	8 pkg.
Warm water (110° to 115°F)	¼ cup	1 cup
Eggs, beaten	4	16
Lemon peel, grated	1 Tbsp.	¼ cup
All-purpose flour, sifted	6 cups	24 cups

Scald milk; stir in ½ cup (2 cups) butter, salt and sugar. Cool to lukewarm.

Sprinkle yeast on warm water; stir to dissolve. Combine eggs and lemon peel and add with yeast to milk mixture. Beat in flour a little at a time, to make a soft dough you can handle. Turn onto floured board; knead lightly until dough is smooth and satiny.

Place in greased bowl; turn dough over to grease top. Cover and let rise in warm place free from drafts until doubled, about 2 hours.

Punch down and turn onto floured board; knead lightly. Shape dough into 1 (4) large ball(s) or into 12 (48) equal balls. Take top quarter of each ball into both hands, pull up and make one complete twist to form the top knob. Place in well-greased brioche pan(s). Brush with melted butter. Cover and let rise about 1 hour.

Preheat oven to 375°F. Bake for 20 to 30 minutes for small brioche or 50 minutes for large, until golden brown. Remove from pan(s) at once. Place on wire rack to cool.

NOTE: Dough may be divided to make a brioche ring plus some individual brioche.

STIR-FRY SPINACH, TOMATO AND BACON

This can be prepared at the table with an electric wok or fry pan.

Ingredients	6 Portions	24 Portions
Spinach, fresh	1 lb.	4 lb.
Bacon	3 slices	12 slices
Onion, small, finely minced	1	4
Garlic clove, finely minced	1	4

Water or chicken stock	2 Tbsp.	½ cup
Cherry tomatoes, halved	1 pint	2 quarts
Tarragon	⅛ tsp.	½ tsp.
Salt	To taste	To taste
Pepper	To taste	To taste

Wash spinach thoroughly, discarding stems; stack leaves and cut crosswise into ½-inch strips. Set aside.

Cook bacon in wok or large frying pan over low heat until crisp; remove and drain. Pour out bacon drippings.

Place pan over high heat and add 2 Tbsp. of the bacon drippings. When hot, add onion and garlic. Stir-fry about 1 minute.

Add spinach and water or stock; stir to mix with onion, cover pan and cook 1 minute or just until spinach is wilted. Add tomatoes, tarragon, salt and pepper. Stir-fry until tomatoes are just hot, about 1 minute. Spoon onto warm plates and sprinkle with crumbled bacon.

Jellied Madrilene
Spinach and Bacon Salad
Swedish Rye Bread
Soufflé Omelet Leonel

•

Jellied Madrilene is amazingly easy to make; serve it plain, with a dab of yogurt or sour cream, or with watercress or diced cucumber as a garnish.

Spinach and Bacon Salad with a hot dressing is perfect with the flavor of Swedish Rye Bread. The bread is so good you hardly need anything more to eat—but some cheese could be added if desired.

Few Americans consider an omelet as dessert fare, probably because they've never tried one. Dessert omelets are almost always flavored with a liqueur, and served with a sauce. Light, airy, sweet and tender—they're a perfect dessert.

JELLIED MADRILENE

A sparkling, refreshing red soup to serve cold.

Ingredients	8 Portions	24 Portions
Tomato puree	3 cups	9 cups
Hot beef or chicken consommé	1 quart	3 quarts
Gelatin	1 oz.	3 oz.
Water, cold	3 Tbsp.	½ cup
Tabasco	Few drops	To taste
Salt	To taste	To taste
Pepper	To taste	To taste
Watercress or cucumber, chopped	½ cup	1½ cups

Pour the puree into a large saucepan over medium heat and cook it until it is reduced to one-third. Add the consommé.

Soften the gelatin in cold water, then stir it into the hot soup. When it is blended take the soup from the pan, cool and leave until set.

Garnish with watercress or diced cucumber.

SWEDISH RYE BREAD

Fat, round, brown loaves sprinkled beautifully with caraway seeds.

Ingredients	3 Loaves	6 Loaves
Dry yeast	1 pkg.	2 pkg.
Warm water	½ cup	1 cup
Rye flour	2 cups	4 cups
Dark molasses	¾ cup	1½ cups
Shortening	⅓ cup	⅔ cup
Salt	2 tsp.	1 Tbsp. + 1 tsp.
Boiling water	2 cups	1 quart
Kummel liqueur, optional	1 Tbsp.	2 Tbsp.
All-purpose flour, unsifted	6 cups or more	12 cups or more
Egg, lightly beaten	1	2
Caraway seeds	2 Tbsp.	¼ cup

Soften yeast in the warm (not boiling) water.

Combine rye flour, molasses, shortening and salt; add boiling water and Kummel. Blend well. Cool to lukewarm. Add softened yeast. Gradually stir in white flour to make a soft dough, mixing well.

Turn onto a well-floured surface and knead until dough is smooth and satiny, about 10 minutes. Place in an oiled bowl and turn to grease the surfaces of the dough.

Cover and let rise in a warm place until double, about 1½ to 2 hours. Punch down. Cover and let rise again.

Preheat oven to 350°F.

Turn dough onto lightly floured surface and divide into 3 (6) equal parts; shape into 3 (6) round loaves. Place on greased baking sheets, brush loaves with oil, and let rise until doubled, about 1 hour.

Brush loaves with lightly beaten egg, sprinkle with caraway seeds, and bake for 35 to 40 minutes.

SOUFFLÉ OMELET LEONEL

We first tasted this at the Houston Club, in Texas.

Ingredients	8 Portions	24 Portions
Eggs, whole	5 small	13 small
Butter	7 Tbsp.	21 Tbsp.
All-purpose flour	½ cup	1½ cups
Milk	1 cup	3 cups
Sugar	½ cup	1½ cups
Grand Marnier	¼ cup	¾ cup
Lemon juice	1 Tbsp.	3 Tbsp.
Confectioners' sugar	2 Tbsp.	6 Tbsp.
Fruit sauce filling (any sweetened crushed or cooked fruit)	1 cup	3 cups

Preheat oven to 375°F.

Separate eggs, putting whites in one bowl and dividing yolks into two bowls of 3 and 2 (8 and 5); set aside.

In a large stainless bowl, melt butter over low heat. When butter melts, add flour and cook for 2 minutes, stirring constantly. Remove from heat and set aside.

In a saucepan, bring milk and sugar to a boil. When sugar is dissolved, pour mixture into stainless bowl containing flour and butter. Mix well, until the consistency is like crepe batter. Add Grand Marnier and egg yolks. Mix well with a wire whip and set aside. (This can be done before lunch.)

In a large mixing bowl, combine 5 (13) egg whites and whip until stiff. Add lemon juice and continue mixing for 2 minutes. Fold this meringue into omelet batter using a rubber spatula.

Divide into greased skillets. Place skillets on level cooking rack and bake 15 minutes.

Remove from oven and place fruit sauce filling in a line down the omelet center; fold omelet along this line. Dust top lightly with confectioners' sugar. Serve with *Sauce Leonel* (recipe follows).

SAUCE LEONEL

Ingredients	8 Portions	24 Portions
Heavy whipping cream	**1 pint**	**3 pints**
Confectioners' sugar	**½ cup + 2 Tbsp.**	**1¾ cup + 2 Tbsp.**
Vanilla extract	**½ tsp.**	**1½ tsp.**
Egg yolks	**2**	**5**
Grand Marnier	**¼ cup**	**¾ cup**

Beat whipping cream until stiff. Beat in remaining ingredients. Serve with soufflé.

4-Fruit Waldorf Salad
Gruyere Quiche Lorraine
Hard Water Roll
Pink Peppermint Crunch Ice Cream

•

Waldorf Salad was indeed invented at the world-famous Wal-
dorf-Astoria Hotel in New York—until the Waldorf's chef
thought of it, no one had combined apples, walnuts, celery and
mayonnaise. This recipe goes that combination one or two
better by adding a variety of fruits—pears, oranges and grapes.

The salad's flavor and texture are excellent with a cheesy Quiche
Lorraine hiding bits of bacon near its crust in the traditional
manner.

Complete the light meal with the fresh flavor of peppermint.
Crush peppermint candy and stir it into softened vanilla or
chocolate ice cream, then refreeze.

4-FRUIT WALDORF SALAD

Makes a picture-pretty platter or individual serving.

Ingredients	8 Portions	24 Portions
Fresh pear, peeled, diced	2 cups	6 cups
Apples, diced	2 cups	6 cups
Celery, thinly sliced	1 cup	3 cups
Lemon juice	2 Tbsp., or to taste	½ cup, or to taste
Sugar	1 tsp.	1 Tbsp.
Mayonnaise	½ cup	1½ cups
Lettuce leaves	8	24
GARNISH		
Orange slices	8	24
Grapes	8 small clusters	24 small clusters
Walnuts, chopped	¼ cup	¾ cup

Combine pears, apples, celery, lemon juice, sugar and mayonnaise. Line plates with lettuce leaf and equally divide fruit mixture.

Garnish each salad with orange slice, grape cluster and chopped walnuts.

GRUYERE QUICHE LORRAINE

The cheese and bacon are layered next to the crust, covered with a tender custard.

Ingredients	1 9-inch Pie	4 9-inch Pies
Bacon	6 thick slices	24 thick slices
Pastry shell	1	4
Gruyere cheese	12 thin slices	48 thin slices
Eggs	4	16
Flour	1 Tbsp.	¼ cup
Nutmeg	¼ tsp.	1 tsp.
Salt	½ tsp.	2 tsp.
Cayenne pepper	Dash	⅛ tsp.
Light cream	1 pint	2 quarts
Butter, melted, cooled	1½ Tbsp.	6 Tbsp.

Preheat oven to 375°F.

Cut bacon slices in half; broil and drain. Cover the pie crust(s) with overlapping pieces of bacon and cheese.

Beat together the eggs, flour, nutmeg, salt and cayenne. Add the cream and melted butter. Pour the custard over the bacon and cheese.

Bake quiche for about 40 minutes, or until custard is set and the top is nicely browned. Best served warm.

Salted Soy Nuts

Springtime Salad

Sherried Mushroom and Chicken-Filled Crepes

Fern's Lemon Pie

•

Springtime Salad is layers of sliced green peppers, red tomatoes, radishes and onion rings with a dill dressing.

The Crepes should be made well ahead; the filling can be held over hot water to fill the warmed crepes at serving time.

Fern's Lemon Pie came to me as a gift from a friend. I tried one piece of it and over the next two days I ate the entire pie myself!

SPRINGTIME SALAD

This is particularly pretty arranged in layers in a glass bowl.

Ingredients	6 Portions	24 Portions
SALAD		
Green pepper rings,	½ cup	2 cups
Radishes, sliced	¾ cup	3 cups
Tomato, sliced	1 cup	4 cups
Onion rings, thinly sliced	1 cup	4 cups
DRESSING		
Soy oil	2 Tbsp.	½ cup
Lemon juice	2 Tbsp.	½ cup
Parsley, chopped	2 tsp.	2 Tbsp. + 2 tsp.
Dry mustard	½ tsp.	2 tsp.
Salt	½ tsp.	2 tsp.
Garlic salt	⅛ tsp.	½ tsp.
Black pepper, freshly ground	⅛ tsp.	½ tsp.
Dill weed, dried	½ tsp.	2 tsp.

SALAD: Layer green pepper rings, radishes, tomato and onion rings.

DRESSING: Shake ingredients together and pour over vegetable mixture. Chill 1 hour.

SHERRIED MUSHROOM AND CHICKEN-FILLED CREPES

Keep the crepes and the sauce warm and put them together just before serving.

Ingredients	6 Portions	24 Portions
Butter	4 Tbsp.	16 Tbsp.
Mushrooms, fresh, sliced	½ lb.	2 lb.
Onions, finely chopped	⅓ cup	1⅓ cups
Flour	¼ cup	1 cup
Milk	2 cups	½ gallon
Chicken bouillon cubes	2	8
Salt	¾ tsp.	1 Tbsp.
White pepper	⅛ tsp.	½ tsp.
Sour cream	½ cup	2 cups
Dry sherry	2 Tbsp.	½ cup
Chicken, boned, cooked, cut in chunks	2 cups	8 cups

Parsley, finely chopped	3 Tbsp.	¾ cup
Crepes (recipe follows)	12	48

Melt butter in a large skillet. Add mushrooms and onions; sauté 5 minutes. Blend in flour; cook and stir over low heat for 2 minutes. Add milk, bouillon cubes, salt and white pepper. Cook and stir over low heat until mixture is thickened. Stir in sour cream and sherry.

Remove 1 cup (4) of the sauce; keep warm. To remaining sauce add chicken and two-thirds of the parsley. Heat just until hot. *Do not boil.*

Meanwhile, heat crepes, tightly covered, in preheated 350°F oven for 10 minutes. Place about ¼ cup mushroom-chicken mixture in each crepe; roll up.

Place 2 filled crepes on each plate. Spoon about 2 Tbsp. of the remaining sauce over each portion. Sprinkle with remaining parsley. Serve immediately.

BASIC CREPES

Make a lot and freeze them—they're wonderful to have on hand for appetizers, entrees or desserts, and they'll help you stretch a little bit of anything.

Ingredients	12 Crepes	48 Crepes
Flour, all-purpose	1¼ cups	5 cups
Salt	⅛ tsp.	½ tsp.
Eggs, beaten	3	12
Milk	1½ cups	1 quart + 2 cups
Butter	2 Tbsp.	½ cup

Place all ingredients in blender or mixer and beat well.
Let batter stand 1 hour for perfect crepes.

NOTE: Chicken or beef bouillon can be substituted for part of the milk.

FERN'S LEMON PIE

This is one of the most unusual pies you'll ever taste—and one of the best.

Ingredients	1 Pie	4 Pies
Lemons	2 large	8 large
Eggs, well-beaten	4	16
Sugar	2 cups	8 cups
Crust for double-crust pie	1 9-inch	4 9-inch

Slice lemons as thin as paper, rind and all; remove seeds. Combine with sugar; mix well. Let stand 2 hours or longer, stirring occasionally.

Preheat oven to 400°F.

Add beaten eggs to lemon mixture; mix well. Turn into pie shell, arranging lemon slices evenly. Cover with top crust. Cut several slits near center.

Bake for 15 minutes. Reduce heat to 375°F and bake for 20 minutes or until knife inserted near edge of pie comes out clean. Cool thoroughly before serving.

Prosciutto or Salmon Coronets
Spinach Frittata
Warm French Bread
Pineapple Shells Deluxe

•

Either salmon or prosciutto can be used to make the pretty appetizer course, which can be passed with drinks before the meal.

Spinach Frittata is a good entree to keep in mind for vegetarian guests.

The Pineapple Shells Deluxe are filled with a pineapple ice cream made from the fruit you scrape from the shells.

PROSCIUTTO or SALMON CORONETS

Sustaining, but not overly rich, and very attractive.

Ingredients	4 Portions	24 Portions
Tuna, canned, with oil	8 oz.	48 oz.
Eggs, hard-cooked	2	12
Mayonnaise	2 Tbsp.	¾ cup
Salt	¼ tsp.	1½ tsp.
Pepper, freshly ground	To taste	To taste
Lemon juice	To taste	To taste
Dill, fresh	1 tsp.	2 Tbsp.
Smoked salmon, thinly sliced	8 slices	48 slices
or	or	or
Prosciutto	4 slices, halved	24 slices, halved

Chop together in the blender tuna and oil, eggs, mayonnaise and seasonings. Spoon mixture onto smoked salmon or prosciutto and roll into a coronet.

Garnish with a sprig of fresh dill. Serve on lettuce leaf with a thin wedge of lemon.

SPINACH FRITTATA

So simple and so foolproof that a child can make it.

Ingredients	4 Portions	24 Portions
Spinach, frozen, chopped	1 pkg. (10 oz.)	6 pkg. (10 oz. ea.)
Butter	3 Tbsp.	1 cup + 2 Tbsp.
Mushrooms, fresh, sliced	½ lb.	3 lb.
or	or	or
Mushrooms, canned	4 oz.	24 oz.
Onion, finely chopped	¼ cup	1½ cups
Eggs, large	6	36
Seasoned salt	½ tsp.	1 Tbsp.
Freshly ground pepper	To taste	To taste
Parmesan cheese, grated	⅓ cup	2 cups
Parsley, optional	As needed	As needed
Red peppers, optional	As needed	As needed

Cook spinach according to package directions. Drain well, pressing out excess water.

Meanwhile, in large ovenproof skillet(s), over medium heat cook mushrooms and onions in butter until tender, but not brown, about 7 to 10 minutes.

Beat together eggs and salt and pepper. Stir in drained spinach. Pour over mushrooms and onions. If using canned mushrooms do not sauté in butter. Add mushrooms with liquid to egg mixture.

Cook over low to medium heat until eggs are set, about 7 minutes. Sprinkle with cheese. Broil about 6 inches from heat for 2 to 3 minutes.

Cut in wedges to serve. Garnish with parsley and peppers, if desired.

PINEAPPLE SHELLS DELUXE

Picture-pretty and a refreshing way to finish a lovely lunch.

Ingredients	4 Portions	24 Portions
Pineapples, fresh	2 small	12 small
Pineapple juice	1¼ cups	7½ cups
Water	¾ cup	4½ cups
Sugar	1 cup + 2 tsp.	6 cups + ¼ cup
Lemon, rind and juice	1 lemon	6 lemons
Heavy cream, whipped	1¼ cups	7½ cups
Kirsch	1 Tbsp.	¼ cup + 2 Tbsp.

Cut pineapples in half lengthwise, leaving on the green top. With a fork and spoon, scrape the flesh and juice into a bowl cutting out and discarding the hard core and being careful not to break through the shell.

Sprinkle the inside of each shell with ½ tsp. sugar and chill until ready to use.

Mash flesh of pineapples thoroughly with a fork. Add pineapple juice, water, remaining sugar and grated lemon rind. Bring to a boil and boil 5 minutes. Strain. Add lemon juice and freeze 4 hours.

Beat mixture with a fork; fold in whipped cream and kirsch. Return to freezer.

Just before serving, spoon mixture into chilled pineapple shells; serve immediately.

Avocado Parfait Madrilene
Lobster Soufflé with Lobster Sauce
Steamed Asparagus
Petits Fours

•

Serve the cold appetizer in a wine or parfait glass with the rosy jellied madrilene in the bottom, the white sour cream and cucumber combination in the center and top it off with the green avocado combination.

The high Lobster Soufflé is an attractive dish. Some of the Lobster Sauce is in the bottom of the soufflé dish and the balance is served on the side.

Cut asparagus stems at an angle, Chinese-fashion—they'll cook very quickly. A hint of Pernod or any other licorice-flavored liqueur will make the asparagus even more interesting. The Pernod flavor is excellent with lobster, as well.

Between the appetizer and the soufflé, this is a rich meal. You may not want any dessert at all, but could pass Petits Fours or candies for those with an insatiable sweet tooth.

AVOCADO PARFAIT MADRILENE

The bottom of the glass holds the red madrilene; the middle layer is the white sour cream and cucumber combination, and the green avocado mixture tops it off.

Ingredients	6 Portions	24 Portions
Consommé Madrilene	1½ cans	6 cans
	(13 oz. ea.)	(13 oz. ea.)
Dairy sour cream	1½ cup	3 pints
Cucumber, diced	⅓ cup	1⅓ cups
White pepper	¾ tsp.	1 Tbsp.
Salt	¾ tsp.	1 Tbsp.
Avocado	1½	6
Lemon or lime juice	3 Tbsp.	¾ cup
Green onion, thinly sliced	2	8
Lemon slices	6	24

Divide Consommé Madrilene between 6 (24) wine or parfait glasses. Chill several hours until firm.

Combine sour cream, cucumber, white pepper and half of the salt; spoon over jellied consommé. (The sour cream mixture should not be combined until serving time, as the moisture content of the cucumbers may cause a slight thinning.)

Mash or sieve avocado and mix with lemon juice, remaining salt and green onion. Spoon over sour cream mixture. Garnish with lemon slices.

LOBSTER SOUFFLÉ with LOBSTER SAUCE

Cognac and white wine flavor the sauce.

Ingredients	1 Soufflé	4 Soufflés
Butter	2 tsp.	3 Tbsp.
Parmesan cheese, grated	1 Tbsp.	¼ cup
LOBSTER SAUCE		
Shallots, chopped	¼ cup	1 cup
Parsley, chopped	2 Tbsp.	½ cup
Butter	4 Tbsp.	1 cup
Lobster meat, cooked, chopped	2 cups	8 cups
Cognac	2 Tbsp. (1 oz.)	½ cup (4 oz.)
Dry white wine	½ cup	2 cups
Heavy cream	1 cup	1 quart

SOUFFLÉ

	4 Tbsp.	1 cup
Butter	4 Tbsp.	1 cup
Flour	¼ cup	1 cup
Milk	¼ cup	1 cup
Egg yolks, beaten	4	16
Swiss, Parmesan or mild		
Cheddar cheese	1 cup	4 cups
Salt	½ tsp.	2 tsp.
Cayenne	⅛ tsp.	½ tsp.
Egg whites	6	24
Cream of tartar	¼ tsp.	1 tsp.

Preheat oven to 350°F.

Prepare 6-cup soufflé dish(es) with a 1-inch or higher collar of aluminum foil. Butter dish(es) and inside rim of collar(s). Sprinkle with Parmesan cheese.

LOBSTER SAUCE: Sauté shallots and parsley in butter; add lobster meat, Cognac, wine and cream. Simmer gently for 15 minutes.

SOUFFLÉ: In another saucepan melt butter, stir in flour to make a roux and slowly stir in milk, eliminating any lumps. Cook until simmering and thickened. Whip a little of the hot mixture into the egg yolks and then add egg yolk mixture to the saucepan.

Add cheese, salt and cayenne, stirring constantly until the cheese has melted. Remove from heat.

Beat egg whites together with cream of tartar until stiff but not dry. Fold egg yolk mixture into egg whites.

Spoon half of lobster sauce mixture into bottom of prepared soufflé dish(es), cover with soufflé mixture and bake 20 minutes at 350°F. Increase temperature to 400°F for 10 minutes longer or until soufflé is golden. Serve immediately with remaining Lobster Sauce.

STEAMED ASPARAGUS

Crisp, yet tender, and full of flavor.

Ingredients	6 Portions	24 Portions
Asparagus, fresh, sliced thin	1½ lb.	6 lb.
Butter	2 Tbsp.	½ cup
Water	¼ cup + 1 Tbsp.	1¼ cup
Salt	To taste	To taste
Black pepper, freshly ground	To taste	To taste
Pernod, optional	1 tsp.	1 Tbsp.

In a large frying pan that has a cover, melt butter over high heat.

Add asparagus and water. Cover and cook at high heat, stirring occasionally, until spears are tender and liquid is evaporated, about 3 to 4 minutes.

Season with salt, pepper, and Pernod (if desired) and serve immediately.

Shrimp-Flavored Chips
Oriental Omelet
Sweet-Sour Sauce
Orange Rounds with Triple Sec and Toasted Coconut

•

I first encountered Shrimp-flavored chips in Indonesia, but they appear to be quite readily available in "gourmet" food shops and in ethnic grocery stores. You just drop them into hot fat and they puff up, airy, crunchy and delicious.

The puffy Oriental Omelet gets its soufflé-like appearance from egg whites and yolks which are beaten separately, then folded together. To ensure proper puffing, be careful not to overbeat the egg whites and dry them out.

The Sweet and Sour Sauce doubles as a vegetable dish with snow peas, water chestnuts and both green and red pepper strips.

Because they are seedless, use navel oranges for the dessert. Remove the rind by cutting, rather than peeling, so that you don't have any membrane left. Slice the oranges into rounds and sprinkle with any orange-flavored liqueur such as Triple Sec or Cointreau. Chill, and at serving time sprinkle with coconut which toasted in the oven while your omelet was finishing.

ORIENTAL OMELET

A fluffy omelet that holds a surprise in its center fold.

Ingredients	4 Portions	24 Portions
Egg whites	4	24
Water	¼ cup	1½ cups
Salt	¼ tsp.	1½ tsp.
Cream of tartar	¼ tsp.	1½ tsp.
Egg yolks	4	24
White pepper	Dash	¼ tsp.
Butter	2 tsp.	2 Tbsp.
Cheddar cheese, shredded	1¼ cups (5 oz.)	7½ cups (30 oz.)

Preheat oven to 325°F.

Beat egg whites, water, salt and cream of tartar until stiff but not dry.

Beat egg yolks and pepper until thick and lemon-colored. Fold beaten yolks into beaten whites.

Melt butter in skillet(s) with heatproof handle(s), until just hot enough to sizzle a drop of water. Turn egg mixture into skillet(s). Cook over low heat on top of range until puffy and browned on bottom (about 5 minutes).

Transfer to oven and bake 12 to 15 minutes or until knife inserted near center comes out clean.

To serve, remove omelet to heated platter. Score down the center with a sharp knife. Spread most of the cheese over half of the omelet; fold omelet and top with remaining cheese.

SWEET-SOUR SAUCE

Ingredients	2 Cups	12 Cups
Water	1 cup	6 cups
Soy sauce	¼ cup	1½ cups
Brown sugar	¼ cup	1½ cups
Vinegar	2 Tbsp.	¾ cup
Cornstarch	2 Tbsp.	¾ cup
Dry mustard	½ tsp.	2 Tbsp.
Butter	2 Tbsp.	¾ cup
Snow peas, fresh or frozen (thawed)	½ cup	3 cups
Water chestnuts, sliced thin	¼ cup	1½ cups
Green pepper, cut in strips	¼ cup	1½ cups
Red pepper, cut in strips	¼ cup	1½ cups

Heat together water, soy sauce, brown sugar, vinegar, cornstarch and dry mustard. Cook over medium heat, stirring constantly, until thickened. Cook 2 additional minutes.

Remove from heat; stir in butter until melted. Add peas, water chestnuts and pepper strips. Keep warm for serving.

To serve, spoon some sauce over omelet and pass remaining sauce with serving.

Swiss Endive Quiche Tarts
Fresh Fruit Plate
Poppy Seed Dressing
Stacked Crepes with Hazelnuts and Chocolate-Rum Sauce

•

Either buy small tart shells or shape your own over the back of a muffin tin. Partially bake them and place on a baking sheet to be filled with the quiche mixture. These tarts can be passed at cocktail parties or served as appetizers, and they make a nice accompaniment for almost any kind of salad or fruit plate.

Poppy Seed Dressing is an old Southern favorite. Most people don't want to add a dressing to a fresh fruit plate, but once they taste this one, they're hooked. It is a nice mixture of sweet and tart and the poppy seeds add crunch.

The crepes can come from your freezer and when you don't have hazelnuts at hand substitute walnuts—black walnuts are particularly nice. Stack up the crepes before the guests arrive, and keep the sauce hot in a double-boiler until serving time.

SWISS ENDIVE QUICHE TARTS

An unusual filling for quiche.

Ingredients	6 Portions	24 Portions
Endive, chopped	1 lb.	4 lb.
Water	½ cup	2 cups
Salt	1 tsp.	1 Tbsp. + 1 tsp.
Butter	3 Tbsp.	¾ cup
Lemon juice	1 tsp.	1 Tbsp. + 1 tsp.
Eggs	3	12
Whipping cream	1½ cup	1 quart + 2 cups
Nutmeg	⅛ tsp.	½ tsp.
Pepper	⅛ tsp.	½ tsp.
Tart shells	6	24
Swiss cheese, grated	¼ cup	1 cup

Preheat oven to 375°F.

Boil endive in water, salt, butter, and lemon juice until liquid is almost evaporated. Lower heat and stew gently for 20 minutes.

Beat eggs, cream and seasonings and gradually add endive. Pour mixture into tart shells and sprinkle with cheese.

Bake for about 20 minutes or until puffed and browned.

POPPY SEED DRESSING

Wonderful with any fruit salad or fruit plate.

Ingredients	1 Pint	½ Gallon
Soy oil	1½ cups	1 quart + 1 cup
Wine vinegar	½ cup	2 cups
White corn syrup	¼ cup + 1 Tbsp.	1¼ cups
Onion, finely grated	¼	1
Dry mustard	½ Tbsp.	2 Tbsp.
Poppy seeds	1½ Tbsp.	¼ cup + 2 Tbsp.

Combine soy oil, vinegar, corn syrup, onion and mustard until the oil disappears.

Add poppy seeds and mix just a few minutes longer. Store in wide-mouth glass or plastic jar in refrigerator.

NOTE: To add color and flavor, maraschino cherry juice or maraschino liqueur may be used for a part of the syrup mixture.

STACKED CREPES with HAZELNUTS

Stack crepes ahead but serve the sauce warm.

Ingredients	6 Portions	24 Portions
Hazelnuts	8 oz.	2 lb.
Soy oil	1 tsp.	1 Tbsp. + 1 tsp.
Confectioners' sugar	½ cup	2 cups
Crepes (see Index)	12	48

Chop hazelnuts coarsely and heat in oil. Add confectioners' sugar and stir until well carmelized.

Stack crepes with nuts topping each crepe. Serve with *Chocolate-Rum Sauce* (recipe follows).

CHOCOLATE-RUM SAUCE

Ingredients	6 Portions	24 Portions
Semi-sweet chocolate	12 oz.	3 lb.
Baking chocolate, unsweetened	2 oz. (or squares)	8 oz. (or squares)
Instant coffee powder	1 Tbsp.	¼ cup
Heavy cream	1 cup	1 quart
Rum	3 Tbsp.	¾ cup

Combine ingredients in a double-boiler over medium heat; stir frequently until chocolate is melted and well combined.

Hot Spiced Tomato Juice
Canadian Egg Pie
Glazed Pineapple
Zucchini Bread

•

Spice up tomato juice with a bit of seasoning salt, hot sauce and
a dash of Worcestershire—then serve it warm with a lemon
wedge. Sip on that while the eggs cook and the cheeses melt
over the Canadian bacon in Canadian Egg Pie.

Top the meal off with Spicy Zucchini Bread made chewy with nuts,
and cups of hot coffee or tea.

CANADIAN EGG PIE

Eggs, bacon and two cheeses, baked to make a pie.

Ingredients	1 Pie	3 Pies
Canadian bacon	10 slices	30 slices
Swiss cheese	8 slices	24 slices
Eggs	8	24
Salt	To taste	To taste
Pepper	To taste	To taste
Half-and-half	1 cup	3 cups
Parmesan cheese, grated	3 Tbsp.	½ cup
Parsley, chopped	1 Tbsp.	3 Tbsp.

Preheat oven to 350°F.

Arrange Canadian bacon around edge of 10-inch pie pan(s). Line bottom with Swiss cheese, slightly overlapping the bacon.

Break eggs separately in small dish. Carefully slide egg out of dish and over the cheese. Sprinkle with salt and pepper. Cover with half-and-half and sprinkle the top with Parmesan cheese and parsley.

Bake for 15 to 20 minutes, until eggs are set and top is light brown. Serve with *Glazed Pineapple* (recipe follows).

GLAZED PINEAPPLE

Apricot and cinnamon add color and flavor.

Ingredients	1 Pie	3 Pies
Pineapple slices	1 can (1 lb., 14 oz.)	3 cans (1 lbs., 14 oz. ea.)
Apricot preserves	½ cup	1½ cups
Butter, melted	2 Tbsp.	6 Tbsp.
Cinnamon	½ tsp.	1½ tsp.

Place pineapple slices in shallow pan, brushing generously with preserves and butter. Sprinkle with cinnamon.

After *Canadian Egg Pie* is baked, broil pineapple for 4 minutes or until hot and bubbly. Serve with pie.

ZUCCHINI BREAD

Spicy—and chewy with nuts.

Ingredients	1 Loaf	2 Loaves
Eggs	2 small	3 large
Sugar	1 cup	2 cups

Soy oil	½ cup	1 cup
Lemon extract	1 tsp.	2 tsp.
Zucchini, grated	1 cup	2 cups
All-purpose flour	1½ cups	3 cups
Baking powder	⅛ tsp.	¼ tsp.
Soda	½ tsp.	1 tsp.
Salt	½ tsp.	1 tsp.
Cinnamon	1 tsp.	2 tsp.
Walnuts or pecans	½ cup	1 cup

Preheat oven to 350°F.

Combine eggs, sugar and oil; beat well. Fold in grated zucchini and lemon extract. Combine dry ingredients and nuts; stir into zucchini mixture. Grease and flour loaf pan(s).

Bake 1 hour.

Pâté Slices with Fanned Cornichon
Watercress-Mushroom Salad
Individual Triple Cheese Soufflés
Hot Biscuits
Blackberry Pie

•

Whether you make your own pâté or purchase it, present it with a sour pickle (cornichon) on a lettuce leaf. Fanning the pickle is done by making thin vertical cuts to, but not through, the end of the pickle, then spreading the slices.

If you don't have individual soufflé dishes, oven-proof soup bowls can be used for the soufflés, or oven-proof cups. The souffles can be made ahead and frozen.

The Blackberry Pie is luscious as is, but even better served warm, topped with whipped cream which has been flavored with Blackberry Brandy. When blackberries are out of season, substitute blueberries (fresh, canned or frozen) and add two teaspoons lemon juice and some Cassis to the recipe.

WATERCRESS-MUSHROOM SALAD

The bitter watercress combines beautifully with the delicate mushrooms.

Ingredients	6 Portions	24 Portions
Watercress leaves	4 cups (2 bunches)	16 cups (8 bunches)
Mushrooms, sliced thin	¼ lb.	1 lb.
DRESSING		
Soy oil	⅓ cup	1⅓ cups
Vinegar, tarragon, white wine or white	2 Tbsp.	½ cup
Salt	¼ tsp.	1 tsp.
Pepper, freshly ground	To taste	To taste

Combine watercress and mushrooms.

Toss with dressing made by combining remaining ingredients. Serve at once.

INDIVIDUAL TRIPLE CHEESE SOUFFLÉS

Under each golden crown, these individual soufflés feature the flavor of cheddar, Swiss and Parmesan cheeses plus a choice of seafood or vegetable.

Ingredients	5 Portions	25 Portions
Parmesan cheese, grated	As needed	As needed
Butter	4 Tbsp.	20 Tbsp.
All-purpose flour	¼ cup	1¼ cups
Salt	¼ tsp.	1¼ tsp.
Cayenne pepper	Dash	¼ tsp.
Milk	1 cup	5 cups
Cheddar cheese, shredded	1 cup (4 oz.)	5 cups (20 oz.)
Swiss cheese, shredded	1 cup (4 oz.)	5 cups (20 oz.)
Parmesan cheese, grated	¼ cup	1¼ cups
Egg yolks, slightly beaten	6	30
Egg whites	6	30
Cream of tartar	¼ tsp.	1¼ tsp.

Preheat oven to 350°F.

Sprinkle enough Parmesan cheese in well-buttered 10-oz. soufflé dishes to coat bottom and sides evenly; remove any excess.

Melt butter; blend in flour, salt and cayenne pepper. Remove from heat; stir in milk. Heat to boiling, stirring constantly. Boil and stir 1 minute.

Remove from heat and stir in cheeses until melted. If necessary, return to low heat to finish melting cheeses. (*Do not boil.*) Blend a little of hot mixture into egg yolks; return all to saucepan and blend thoroughly. Transfer sauce to large bowl.

In a small mixing bowl beat egg whites until foamy. Add cream of tartar and beat until soft peaks form. Fold egg whites into cheese sauce. Turn mixture into soufflé dishes, filling three-fourths full.

Bake one or more soufflés for 30–35 minutes. Serve immediately.

VARIATION: Add chopped cooked poultry or seafood or chopped, cooked, well-drained broccoli or spinach to the egg/cheese mixture and fill soufflé dishes three-fourths full.

FREEZING: Carefully wrap any remaining unbaked soufflés in freezer wrap and freeze up to 1 month. To bake frozen soufflé, unwrap and place directly from freezer into preheated 300°F oven for about 1 hour + 10 minutes.

BLACKBERRY PIE

Serve warm and fresh from the oven.

Ingredients	1 Pie	4 Pies
Sugar	⅔ cup	2⅔ cup
All-purpose flour	¼ cup	1 cup
Cinnamon	½ tsp.	2 tsp.
Lemon peel, grated	½ tsp.	2 tsp.
Nutmeg	¼ tsp.	1 tsp.
Salt	⅛ tsp.	½ tsp.
Blackberries	5 cups	20 cups
Pastry for double-crust pie	one 9-in.	four 9-in.
Butter or margarine	1 Tbsp.	4 Tbsp.
Heavy cream	½ pint	1 quart
Blackberry flavored brandy	1 Tbsp.	¼ cup

Preheat oven to 425°F.

In large bowl, combine sugar, flour, cinnamon, lemon peel, nutmeg and salt; add berries and toss well; set aside.

Spoon berry filling evenly into unbaked pie crust(s); dot with butter or margarine. Cover with top crust(s) and brush lightly with milk. Bake 50 minutes or until golden.

Whip cream and add brandy to cream and pass with hot pie.

Peasant Soup
Confetti Sandwiches on
English Muffins
Peach Slices in Red Wine

•

Potatoes and leeks are both traditional peasant fare, but when they're combined in a soup with chicken stock and half-and-half, they're fit for a king.

You should never cut an English muffin with a knife; instead use two forks to pull apart, leaving nice rough peaks and valleys.

Topping the toasted muffins is a recipe that won an award in the National Sandwich Idea Contest. It is healthy, hearty and most attractive with spinach, carrots, olives and hard-cooked eggs, held together with sour cream, then topped with cheese and bacon bits. Serve the sandwich open face to brighten the soup.

Peaches served in a wine glass with red wine are a pleasant way to finish the meal. The peaches could be fresh, frozen or canned. Garnish with a cinnamon stick.

PEASANT SOUP

Serve it with chunks of potatoes and leeks, or puree for a smooth consistency.

Ingredients	6 Portions	24 Portions
Leeks, medium	3	12
Butter	1 Tbsp.	4 Tbsp.
Potatoes	1 lb.	4 lb.
Chicken stock	1 quart	1 gallon
Half-and-half	¼ cup	1 cup
Salt	To taste	To taste
White pepper	To taste	To taste
Nutmeg	⅛ tsp.	½ tsp.
Chives, chopped	2 Tbsp.	½ cup
or	or	or
Scallion tops, chopped	¼ cup	1 cup

Wash the leeks very thoroughly and discard the tough part of the green tops. Cut in thin slices and again rinse, draining well.

Cook leeks in butter until soft. Add diced potatoes and chicken stock; simmer about 30 minutes. Add half-and-half, salt, pepper and nutmeg. Sprinkle with chives or scallions.

This soup may be whirled in a blender to make a puree. If it becomes too thick, adjust consistency by adding stock or half-and-half.

CONFETTI SANDWICHES

So attractive you would never guess that they're brimming with nutrients!

Ingredients	6 Portions	24 Portions
Eggs, hard-cooked, chopped	9	36
Sour cream	½ cup	2 cups
Black pepper, freshly ground	To taste	To taste
Fresh spinach, chopped	⅓ cup	1⅓ cups
Carrot, shredded	¼ cup	1 cup
Green onions, chopped	¼ cup	1 cup
Ripe olives, pitted, chopped	¼ cup	1 cup
English Muffins (recipe follows)	6	24
Butter	¼ cup	1 cup
Cheddar cheese, shredded	1 cup	4 cups
Bacon, cooked, crumbled	6 slices	24 slices

Preheat oven to broil.

Combine eggs, sour cream, pepper, vegetables and olives.

Split, toast and butter muffins. Spread egg mixture over top of each half muffin. Sprinkle with shredded cheese and bacon.

Broil 6 inches from heat until cheese melts, about 3 to 5 minutes. Serve open faced.

ENGLISH MUFFINS

English muffins aren't baked in the oven, they're fried.

Ingredients	12 Muffins	24 Muffins
Milk, scalded	1 cup	2 cups
Butter	3 Tbsp.	6 Tbsp.
Sugar	2 Tbsp.	1/4 cup
Salt	1 1/4 tsp.	2 1/2 tsp.
Yeast, cake or dry	1	2
Water, lukewarm	1/4 cup	1/2 cup
Egg, beaten	1	2
Flour, all-purpose	4 cups	8 cups
Bran	1/4 cup	1/2 cup
Corn meal	As needed	As needed

Combine milk, butter, sugar and salt.

Soften yeast in lukewarm water. Add yeast, egg and 2 (4) cups of the flour to the milk mixture. Stir to blend well. Then knead in the remaining flour and bran until smooth and elastic. Cover. Let rise in a warm place until double in bulk, about 1 hour.

Roll out 1/4 inch thick on a floured board. Cut into 4-inch circles. Cover and let rise until doubled in bulk, about 1 hour.

When light, sprinkle with corn meal, if desired, and cook slowly on ungreased heavy griddle or frying pan, about 7 minutes on each side.

Broiled Grapefruit with Rum
Avocado Omelet with Avocado Sauce
Walnut Danish Pastries

•

Broiling grapefruit completely changes its character—when the heat's on grapefruit grows mellow. Divide the fruit in two with a zig-zag cut, rather than a straight one. Sprinkle on a little brown sugar and a bit of rum and broil until it is heated through and the peaks begin to brown.

Avocado Omelet harbors diced avocado meat in its center fold. The Avocado Sauce is based upon bacon and tomatoes with a dash of chili powder for spice and mashed avocado for substance.

The breadstuff also serves as dessert. Walnut Danish Pastries can be made three ways, each one better than the last.

AVOCADO OMELET with AVOCADO SAUCE

Lovers of hot Mexican food may wish to add a few drops of hot sauce or chopped Jalapeno pepper to both the omelet and the Avocado Sauce.

Ingredients	6 Portions	24 Portions
Eggs	9	3 dozen
Milk	½ cup + 1 Tbsp.	2¼ cups
Salt	To taste	To taste
Pepper	To taste	To taste
Butter	3 Tbsp.	12 Tbsp.
Avocados	1½	6

Prepare omelet (see Omelet Hints), then arrange avocado chunks across center of omelet. Fold over sides and remove to warm platter. Serve with *Avocado Sauce* (recipe follows).

AVOCADO SAUCE

Ingredients	6 Portions	24 Portions
Bacon, chopped	6 slices	24 slices
Onion, diced	1 medium	4 medium
Tomatoes, diced	3 large	12 large
Salt	To taste	To taste
Pepper	To taste	To taste
Chili powder	¼ tsp.	1 tsp.
Avocados	3	12

In medium skillet, cook bacon until almost done; pour off about half of bacon grease. Add onions, tomatoes, salt, pepper and chili powder. Simmer several minutes or until onion is soft. Remove from heat.

Meanwhile, peel avocados (reserve 4 or 5 slices for garnish); mash remaining avocados and add to sauce.

Serve in pitcher or gravy boat or pour onto omelet.

OMELET HINTS

TO PREPARE OMELET: Mix eggs, water, salt and pepper with fork. Heat butter in 10-inch omelet pan or skillet until just hot enough to sizzle a drop of water. Pour in egg mixture. Mixture should set at edges at once. With pancake turner, carefully draw cooked portions at edges toward center, so uncooked portions flow to bottom. Tilt skillet as needed to hasten flow of uncooked eggs. Slide pan rapidly back and forth over heat to keep mixture in motion and sliding freely.

Keep the pan moving at all times. Move it back and forth on the burner with one hand and with the other stir the egg mixture with the back of a fork—you want the eggs to set, but not to stick. As soon as the bottom is firm, add filling, then fold. The omelet will continue to cook a bit as it stands.

THE ENVELOPE OR "CLASSIC" FOLD: While still moist on top, but firmly set, fold nearest side one-third over the center, bring the back third over that and flip over onto the warmed serving plate.

NOTE: Clarified butter (butter that has been melted so that the milk solids settle to the bottom and the butter fat can be poured off) is best to prevent sticking. If you use regular butter (and you certainly may), don't allow the butter to melt completely before adding the eggs, but do see that the pan bottom is covered with the fat.

WALNUT DANISH PASTRIES

This is an easy recipe for beginning bread makers as you can use hot roll mix. Experienced cooks may prefer to use a basic yeast dough.

DANISH PASTRY

Ingredients	3 dozen	6 dozen
Butter or margarine	1 cup	2 cups
Hot roll mix	1 pkg. (13¾ oz.)	2 pkg. (13¾ oz.)
Warm water	¾ cup	1½ cups
Egg	1	2
Granulated sugar	¼ cup	½ cup
Powdered cardamom	⅛ tsp.	¼ tsp.

Shape butter into a rectangle about 8x10 inches on sheet of waxed paper. Chill thoroughly.

Dissolve yeast from hot roll mix in warm water.

Beat egg lightly; add sugar, cardamom and yeast mixture. Gradually blend in hot roll mix to make a stiff dough. Turn out onto floured board and knead until smooth. Cover dough with a bowl and let rest for 10 minutes.

Roll to a thin rectangle about 11x17 inches. Place chilled butter on one end of dough, leaving a narrow margin of dough at edges of butter. Fold margin of dough over to completely enclose butter. Give dough a quarter turn on board, and roll again to about 12x16 inches. Fold in thirds, wrap in clear plastic film or waxed paper and chill for 20 minutes.

Roll and fold three more times, chilling between each step. Chill again before shaping (it may be wrapped well and refrigerated for 2 to 3 days before shaping and baking, if desired).

HONEY WALNUT FILLING

Ingredients	3 dozen	6 dozen
Honey	3 Tbsp.	6 Tbsp.
California walnuts, finely chopped	½ cup	1 cup
Salt	⅛ tsp.	¼ tsp.
Egg yolk	1	2
Lemon peel, grated	½ tsp.	1 tsp.

Simmer honey, walnuts and salt over low heat about 3 minutes, stirring constantly.

Slowly stir in lightly beaten egg yolk; cook, stirring until lightly thickened. Add lemon peel.

Cool before using.

WALNUT MERINGUE FILLING

Ingredients	3 Dozen	6 Dozen
Egg white	1	2
Salt	⅛ tsp.	¼ tsp.
Granulated sugar	⅓ cup	⅔ cup
California walnuts, grated or finely ground	½ cup	1 cup
Vanilla	½ tsp.	1 tsp.

Beat egg white with salt until stiff. Gradually beat in sugar. Fold in walnuts and vanilla.

WALNUT GLAZE

Ingredients	3 Dozen	6 Dozen
Powdered sugar, sifted	1 cup	2 cups
Milk	1½ Tbsp.	3 Tbsp.
California walnuts, finely chopped	⅓ cup	⅔ cup
Vanilla	¼ tsp.	½ tsp.

Mix all ingredients together well.
Use to glaze pastries.

HONEY WALNUT TWISTS

Cut Danish pastry into 3 (6) equal parts. Roll one-third to a thin rectangle about 7x16 inches. Spread *Honey Walnut Filling* down center of dough. Fold edges over filling, lapping them slightly. Flatten slightly with rolling pin. Cut into 12 strips crosswise. Place about 2 inches apart on lightly greased baking sheet, giving each strip a twist and pressing ends against pan. Let rise 20 to 30 minutes in warm place, until dough feels light when touched. Bake on upper shelf of oven at 400°F, 15 to 20 minutes, until nicely browned. Remove to wire rack to cool.

DIAMONDS

Roll one-third of Danish pastry to strip about 5x24 inches. Spread half of *Walnut Meringue Filling* on one side of strip, moisten edges and fold over to make a strip about 2½x24 inches long. Cut in half for ease of handling, and transfer to baking sheet. Let rise and bake as above. Cool slightly, and cut into diamond shapes. Frost with *Walnut Glaze* while warm.

WALNUT CRESCENTS

Roll remaining third of dough to a strip about 7x16 inches. Let rest a few minutes, then cut into triangles. Spread each with a teaspoon of the *Walnut Meringue Filling,* and roll up from broad end of triangle. Place point down on lightly greased baking sheet. Let rise and bake as above. Frost while warm with *Walnut Glaze.*

THREE
For the Calorie Conscious

Everyone is calorie conscious—even the skinny everyones. A chef at a private Boston women's club once told me that his "ladies say they are dieting and only want a fruit plate or a salad, but try leaving the avocado mousse off the menu and you realize that talking dieting and practicing dieting are two different things."

Where weight control is concerned, there is no such thing as a miracle. It is purely and simply a matter of eating fewer calories than you use each day. But fewer calories needn't mean starvation—in fact it can and should mean some interesting food combinations, and sometimes plenty of food.

Complex carbohydrate—the starch form found in breads, cereals, potatoes, etc.—is a handy tool to use in appetite control. Use it to fill your nooks and crannies while you're cutting down on fats which ounce-per-ounce have more than two times the calories found in starch and protein.

What you must have, of course, is a balanced diet—a daily supply of the protein foods (fish, poultry, meat, cheese, eggs, peas, beans or nuts), fruits and vegetables (the rule of thumb is still a daily minimum of two fruits—one a citrus fruit, tomatoes, berries or melon for vitamin C) and two vegetables (one leafy, green or yellow to provide vitamin A).

You need some dairy products for calcium—skim milk is as good a source of calcium as whole milk—and you need cereal grains in some form (usually bread).

You don't have to starve. You simply must choose the foods to eat wisely and well.

Chilled Cucumber and Spinach Soup
62 CALORIES/SERVING

Chicken Paprika with Noodles
280 CALORIES/SERVING

Steamed Broccoli
20 CALORIES/1/2 CUP SERVING

Baked Warm Lemon Pudding
115 CALORIES/SERVING

•

There is buttermilk in both the Chilled Cucumber and Spinach Soup and in the Chicken Paprika. Leftover buttermilk can be substituted for sour cream in your favorite recipes—at a vast reduction in calories.

Chicken Paprika is made with chicken breasts for dieters, but you can add thighs for those who don't have to count calories. The recipe calls for cooked noodles and if your package doesn't tell you, it will take about 1½ cups of uncooked noodles to yield 2 cups of cooked—5⅓ cups of uncooked should produce about 8 cups cooked.

When they're in season, garnish the dessert with a few fresh strawberries or blueberries.

Total calories per person: 477.

CHILLED CUCUMBER AND SPINACH SOUP

62 CALORIES/SERVING
A cool green appetizer.

Ingredients	6 Portions	24 Portions
Scallions, sliced	½ bunch	2 bunches
Butter	1 tsp.	1 Tbsp. +1 tsp.
Cucumbers, sliced	2 cups	8 cups
Spinach, chopped	½ cup	2 cups
Potatoes, sliced	¼ cup	1 cup
Chicken stock	1½ cups	6 cups
Buttermilk	½ cup	2 cups
Lemon juice	½ lemon	2 lemons
Salt	To taste	To taste
Pepper	To taste	To taste

Sauté sliced scallions in butter until they are soft; add vegetables and stock and cook until vegetables are tender.

Transfer to a blender in batches, or to food processor and puree. Refrigerate.

Serve garnished with sliced radish, diced cucumber and chopped greens of scallions.

CHICKEN PAPRIKA with NOODLES

280 CALORIES/SERVING
Only 280 calories per portion when made with buttermilk, nearly double that when sour cream is used.

Ingredients	6 Portions	24 Portions
Chicken half-breasts	6	24
Salt	1½ tsp.	2 Tbsp.
Paprika	1½ tsp.	2 Tbsp.
Pepper	½ tsp.	2 tsp.
Flour	¼ cup	1 cup
Soy oil	2 Tbsp.	½ cup
Onions, diced	¼ cup	1 cup
Hot water	¾ cup	3 cups
Flour	3 Tbsp.	¾ cup
Cultured buttermilk	1½ cups	6 cups
Cooked noodles	2 cups	8 cups
Paprika	1 Tbsp.	¼ cup

Remove bones, skin and excess fat from chicken. Cut pieces in half. Season chicken with salt, paprika and pepper. Roll in flour. Brown slowly in hot oil, 10 to 15 minutes. Add onions, hot water, and lemon juice.

Cook, covered, over low heat about 40 minutes or until chicken is tender. Skim off any excess fat.

Blend 3 Tbsp. (¾ cup) flour with ½ cup (2 cups) of buttermilk. Stir into chicken mixture.

Stir in remaining buttermilk and noodles. Simmer, uncovered, 5 minutes. Add paprika and mix well.

BAKED WARM LEMON PUDDING

115 CALORIES/SERVING
A pudding that makes its own sauce as it bakes.

Ingredients	6 Portions	24 Portions
Egg whites	2	8
Salt	¼ tsp.	1 tsp.
Granulated sugar	¼ cup + 2 Tbsp.	1½ cups
Egg yolks	2	8
Grated lemon peel	1 Tbsp.	¼ cup
Lemon juice	1½ Tbsp.	¼ cup + 2 Tbsp.
Melted butter or margarine	1 Tbsp.	¼ cup
Flour	2 Tbsp.	½ cup
Skim milk	1 cup	4 cups

Preheat oven to 350°F.

Grease 1 quart casserole (4). Beat egg whites with salt until moist peaks form. Gradually add ¼ cup (1 cup) sugar, beating until stiff.

With same beater, beat yolks with lemon peel, lemon juice, and melted butter until blended. Stir in remaining sugar mixed with flour. Add milk. Fold into beaten egg whites.

Pour batter into greased casserole. Set in pan containing ½ inch hot water. Bake, uncovered, 55 to 65 minutes, or until top of pudding is firm and browned. (Pudding will separate into cake layer and sauce layer.)

Serve slightly warm or chilled. Garnish with berries, or other fruit if desired.

Triple Herbed Broth
22 CALORIES/SERVING

Hot Popovers or Corn Sticks
93 CALORIES/SERVING

Tuna and Citrus Spinach Salad
174 CALORIES/SERVING

Lemon Cloud with Blueberry Sauce
76 CALORIES/SERVING

•

The quick and easy broth is a recipe you'll make often. You can use homemade beef stock, canned broth or even bouillon cubes, as a base. Hot popovers or corn sticks add a bit of substance without inordinate calories (particularly if you don't use any spread).

The Tuna and Citrus Spinach Salad is a delight—the juice from the fruit is the base for the dressing, and it can all be prepared ahead—just add the spinach at the last minute and toss at the table.

The dessert is a molded tangy, lemon gelatin, light as a cloud, with a Blueberry Sauce flavored with Cassis.

Total calories per person: 365.

TRIPLE HERBED BROTH

22 CALORIES/SERVING
A one-minute wonder.

Ingredients	6 Portions	24 Portions
Beef broth	1¼ cups	5 cups
Tomato juice	1 cup	4 cups
Water	½ cup	2 cups
Tomato, chopped	1	4
Basil, fresh*	¾ tsp.	1 Tbsp.
Oregano, fresh*	½ tsp.	2 tsp.
Tarragon, fresh*	¼ tsp.	1 tsp.
Parsley, chopped	2 Tbsp.	½ cup

*Use ¼ as much dried

Combine broth, juice, water, tomato, basil, oregano, and tarragon. Bring to a boil, reduce heat and simmer for 1 minute.

Pour into bowls and garnish with parsley.

TUNA AND CITRUS SPINACH SALAD

174 CALORIES/SERVING
Very light in calories but very high in nutrients.

Ingredients	6 Portions	24 Portions
White grapefruit	1½	6
Oranges	3	12
Red wine vinegar	¾ cup	3 cups
Red onion, sliced	1½ cups	6 cups
Pitted ripe olives, sliced	18	72
Tuna packed in water, drained	3 cans (3½ oz. ea.)	12 cans (42 oz.)
Spinach leaves, shredded	6 cups	24 cups

Peel grapefruit and oranges, and section into bowl to catch juices. Add vinegar, onion slices, olives and tuna.

Let mixture marinate under refrigeration. Toss mixture with spinach just prior to serving.

LEMON CLOUD WITH BLUEBERRY SAUCE

76 CALORIES/SERVING

Lemon and blueberries are a hard combination to beat.

Ingredients	8 Portions	24 Portions
Lemon gelatin	1 pkg. (3 oz. ea.)	3 pkg. (3 oz. ea.)
Boiling water	1 cup	3 cups
Lemon peel, grated	1 tsp.	1 Tbsp.
Lemon juice	2 Tbsp.	1/4 cup + 2 Tbsp.
Cold water	3/4 cup	2 1/4 cups
Egg whites	2	6

In large bowl, dissolve gelatin in boiling water. Stir in lemon peel, juice and cold water; chill until partially set.

Add unbeaten egg whites to gelatin mixture. Beat with electric mixer until light and fluffy.

Pour into custard cups. Chill until firm.

To serve, unmold lemon cloud onto individual dessert dishes. Spoon *Blueberry Sauce* (recipe follows) over each dessert.

BLUEBERRY SAUCE

Ingredients	8 Portions	24 Portions
Blueberries	1 1/2 cups	4 1/2 cups
Cornstarch	1 Tbsp.	3 Tbsp.
Cold water	1/2 cup	1 1/2 cups
Sugar	1 Tbsp.	3 Tbsp.
Cassis	1 tsp.	1 Tbsp.

In saucepan, crush one-third of the blueberries. Blend together cornstarch and cold water. Add cornstarch mixture and sugar to crushed blueberries.

Cook over medium heat, stirring constantly, until mixture is thick and bubbly; remove sauce from heat and stir in remaining blueberries and Cassis. Chill.

Toasted Pumpkin Seeds

20 CALORIES/TABLESPOON

Cauliflower with Wine

315 CALORIES/SERVING

Ham and Broccoli Birds in Mustard Sauce

196 CALORIES/SERVING

Whole Wheat Dilly Onion Biscuits

80 CALORIES/BISCUIT

Ice Cold Watermelon Balls

115 CALORIES/SERVING

•

If you have fresh pumpkin seeds, parboil them in salted water, both to salt the seeds and to make it easier to remove the stringy ties that bind the seeds. Once the seeds are free of pumpkin, roast them in the oven and serve as a low-calorie appetizer.

The Ham and Broccoli Birds in Mustard Sauce add enough color so that the white cauliflower can survive on the same plate. Though broccoli and cauliflower are from the same family of vegetables, the different preparations make them taste entirely different.

Fill up on the biscuits (but not on butter), then top it all off with chilled melon balls.

Total calories per person: 726.

CAULIFLOWER with WINE

315 CALORIES/SERVING

This dish can be served as a soup with lots of the wine sauce, or as a vegetable with just a little sauce and bigger flowerets.

Ingredients	6 Portions	24 Portions
Firm white cauliflower	1 large head	4 large heads
Dry white wine	½ cup	2 cups
Soy oil	¼ cup	1 cup
Shallots, finely chopped	2 to 3	8 to 12
Garlic cloves	2	8
Parsley sprigs	6	24
Bay leaves	2	8
Lemon juice	1 lemon	4 lemons
Fennel	1 tsp.	1 Tbsp. + 1 tsp.
Basil	1 tsp.	1 Tbsp. + 1 tsp.
Coriander	1 tsp.	1 Tbsp. + 1 tsp.
Celery seed	¼ tsp.	1 tsp.
Beef stock	2 cups	½ gallon
Salt	½ tsp.	2 tsp.
White pepper	½ tsp.	2 tsp.
Dill weed	¼ tsp.	1 tsp.
Mustard seed	¼ tsp.	1 tsp.

Break cauliflower into small flowerets and blanch for 1 minute in rapidly boiling water. Then drain and run cold water over it immediately, to keep the cauliflower white.

Place remaining ingredients in flat pan, cover and simmer 15 minutes. Taste and correct seasoning.

Add cauliflowerets and more beef stock or white wine (or both) to the pan until cauliflower is three-fourths covered. Replace cover on pan and cook slowly until tender, about 15 to 20 minutes. Turn heat off and let vegetable cool in liquid.

Remove to a serving bowl together with a good deal of stock; chill well. Sprinkle with chopped parsley.

HAM AND BROCCOLI BIRDS IN MUSTARD SAUCE

196 CALORIES/SERVING

Ham rolled around broccoli spears then baked with a coating of mustard sauce.

Ingredients	6 Portions	24 Portions
Broccoli spears, cooked	6 large spears	24 large spears
Ham, thinly sliced	6 oz.	1½ lb.

	1 Tbsp.	¼ cup
Butter	1 Tbsp.	¼ cup
Flour	2 Tbsp.	½ cup
Dry mustard	2 tsp.	2 Tbsp. + 2 tsp.
Celery seed	¼ tsp.	1 Tbsp. + 1 tsp.
Skim milk	1½ cups	6 cups
Salt	To taste	To taste
Pepper	To taste	To taste
Paprika	½ tsp.	2 tsp.
Parsley sprigs	6	24

Preheat oven to 450°F.

Place a broccoli spear in middle of each ham slice. Roll up tightly and arrange, seam side down, in shallow baking dish.

Melt butter and blend in flour, mustard and celery seed. Cook, stirring, 1 to 2 minutes. Slowly add milk and bring to a boil, stirring until smooth and thickened. Season with salt and pepper. Pour onto ham rolls and sprinkle lightly with paprika.

Bake 10 minutes or until hot. Garnish with parsley sprig.

WHOLE WHEAT DILLY ONION BISCUITS

80 CALORIES/BISCUIT

Whole wheat baking powder biscuits flavored with dill, then cut larger than usual.

Ingredients	8 Biscuits	24 Biscuits
Whole wheat flour	1 cup	3 cups
Baking powder	2 tsp.	2 Tbsp.
Salt	½ tsp.	1½ tsp.
Minced onion	1 Tbsp.	3 Tbsp.
Dill weed	½ tsp.	1½ tsp.
Margarine	3 Tbsp.	9 Tbsp.
Skim milk	¾ cup	2¼ cups

Preheat oven to 450°F.

In a mixing bowl sift together flour, baking powder, salt, onion, and dill weed. Cut margarine in until mixture looks like coarse meal. Blend in milk. Place dough on a lightly floured surface and knead about 25 times.

Roll dough out to about ½-inch thickness. Cut with 2-inch round biscuit cutter.

Place biscuits on an ungreased cookie sheet and bake about 15 to 20 minutes. Serve hot.

Green and Ripe Olives
8 CALORIES EACH

Eggplant Salad
3 CALORIES/TABLESPOON

Colorful Garden Sandwiches
190 CALORIES/SERVING

Low-Fat Date Bars
145 CALORIES/SERVING

Skim Milk
105 CALORIES/CUP

•

The Eggplant Salad can serve as an appetizer rather than accompanying the sandwiches—whichever you prefer.

We don't think of any cookie as being low in calories, and they're not. But, Low-Fat Date Bars should be allowed now and then, particularly when you're entertaining.

Total calories per person: 451.

EGGPLANT SALAD

3 CALORIES/TABLESPOON

Eggplant is very low in calories and seldom eaten raw. Try it; most people who do, like it.

Ingredients	8 Cups	16 Cups
Raw eggplant, peeled, finely chopped	2 cups	4 cups
Green pepper, minced	½ cup	1 cup
Green onion, minced	½ cup	1 cup
Celery, chopped	1 cup	2 cups
Low-calorie Italian dressing, bottled	½ cup	1 cup
Lemon juice	2 Tbsp.	¼ cup
Pimiento, chopped	¼ cup	½ cup
Parsley, chopped	¼ cup	½ cup
Boston lettuce cups	As needed	As needed

Toss all ingredients, except lettuce, together and chill.
Serve in individual Boston lettuce cups.

COLORFUL GARDEN SANDWICHES

190 CALORIES/SANDWICH

Healthy-looking, good-tasting sandwiches which can utilize almost anything from your garden.

Ingredients	6 Portions	24 Portions
Uncreamed cottage cheese	1 lb.	4 lb.
Watercress, chopped	½ cup	2 cups
Onion, chopped	2 Tbsp.	½ cup
Celery, chopped	¼ cup	1 cup
Tomato, chopped	1 cup	4 cups
Lemon juice	2 tsp.	2 Tbsp. + 2 tsp.
Salt	½ tsp.	2 tsp.
White pepper	½ tsp.	2 tsp.
Sprouted wheat bread, toasted	12 slices	48 slices
Sliced radishes	3	12
Cucumber, sliced	2	8

Combine cottage cheese, tomatoes, watercress, onion, celery, lemon juice, salt and pepper. Chill for 10 minutes.

On half of the bread slices, spread cottage cheese mixture, using about ⅓ cup per slice. Top with radishes and cucumber slices. Cover with toasted bread.

LOW-FAT DATE BARS

145 CALORIES EACH
Rolled oats top and bottom make these filled cookie bars.

Ingredients	24 Bars
BARS	
All-purpose flour	1½ cups
Baking soda	1 tsp.
Salt	¼ tsp.
Rolled oats or wheat	1¼ cups
Brown sugar	1 cup
Melted margarine	⅓ cup
Skim milk	3 Tbsp.
FILLING	
Pitted dates, chopped	1 pkg.
Sugar	½ cup
Flour	1 tsp.
Water	1 cup
Vanilla	1 tsp.

Preheat oven to 350°F.

Combine filling ingredients in a saucepan and cook until thick. Cool.

Combine bar ingredients and pack half into a teflon-coated (or lightly oiled) 9-inch square pan.

Spread cooled filling over the flour mixture and sprinkle remaining half of cake mixture evenly over filling, patting it down.

Bake until golden, about 30 minutes.

Iced Watercress Soup
146 CALORIES/SERVING

Chicken and Artichoke Cup
225 CALORIES/SERVING

Banana Tea Bread
123 CALORIES/SERVING

●

The secret to avoiding an undertaste of bitterness in watercress soup is to use the leaves only—it is the stems that add the bitter flavor. Buttermilk is the low-calorie base for this green beauty.

The Chicken and Artichoke Cup has extra interest because the artichoke hearts are cooked and then chilled in a marinade.

Liquid non-sugar sweetener accounts for the low calorie count in the Banana Tea Bread.

Total calories per person: 494.

ICED WATERCRESS SOUP

146 CALORIES/SERVING

Soup can be an elegant start to any meal; buttermilk gives this one a tangy taste.

Ingredients	6 Portions	24 Portions
Watercress	1 bunch (2 cups)	4 bunches (8 cups)
Soy oil	2 Tbsp.	½ cup
Onions	1 large	4 large
Salt	½ Tbsp.	2 Tbsp.
White pepper	¼ tsp.	1 tsp.
Flour	1 Tbsp.	¼ cup
Chicken broth	2½ cups	10 cups
Nutmeg	¼ tsp.	1 tsp.
Tarragon	½ tsp.	2 tsp.
Dill weed	½ tsp.	2 tsp.
Buttermilk	2 cups	½ gallon
Lemon juice	1 Tbsp.	¼ cup
Worcestershire sauce	½ tsp.	2 tsp.
Curry powder	¼ tsp.	1 tsp.

Wash watercress and remove stems, reserving several of the nicest leaves for use as a garnish.

Heat the oil in a heavy pot and add the onions. Cover and cook slowly until translucent. Add watercress, sprinkle on salt and stir well. Cover and cook slowly for 10 minutes or until cress wilts.

Sprinkle on flour and mix well again. Cover and cook for another 2 minutes. Add chicken broth and pepper. Cover and simmer for 30 minutes. For the last five minutes of cooking add tarragon, dill weed and nutmeg. Let cool slightly.

Ladle part of cress and broth into blender and pour in one cup of buttermilk, the lemon juice and the Worcestershire sauce; blend until smooth. Pour this portion into a large bowl and repeat blending process until all of the soup stock and buttermilk have been used.

Return the soup to the pot and taste for seasoning; correct if necessary. Add curry and heat through.

Chill until thoroughly cold.

A nice garnish can be made simply by dropping reserved watercress leaves onto each bowl of soup.

CHICKEN AND ARTICHOKE CUP

225 CALORIES/SERVING

Artichoke hearts marinate in an Italian dressing before being tossed with the chicken and served on a bed of romaine and spinach.

Ingredients	6 Portions	24 Portions
Low-calorie Italian dressing, bottled	¾ cup	3 cups
Lemon juice	2 Tbsp.	½ cup
Onion, chopped	¼ cup	1 cup
Garlic clove, crushed	1	4
Celery seed	¼ tsp.	1 tsp.
Mustard seed	¼ tsp.	1 tsp.
Salt	½ tsp.	2 tsp.
Pepper	½ tsp.	2 tsp.
Frozen artichoke hearts	9 oz.	2¼ lb.
Tomato	1	4
Chicken breasts, boned, cooked, chilled	2 lb.	8 lb.
Romaine lettuce	2 cups	8 cups
Fresh spinach	3 cups	12 cups

In saucepan combine Italian salad dressing, lemon juice, onion, garlic, celery seed, mustard seed, salt, pepper.

Bring to a boil; add frozen artichoke hearts. Cook until tender, about 3 to 5 minutes; chill. Add tomato wedges and chicken breasts cut into julienne strips.

At serving time drain chilled artichoke mixture, reserving the marinade. Cut artichokes into bite-size pieces if desired. Toss artichoke mixture with chicken strips, torn greens and enough of the reserved marinade to coat the greens.

BANANA TEA BREAD

123 CALORIES/SERVING

Ingredients	1 Loaf (12 servings)	2 Loaves (24 servings)
Sifted flour	1¾ cups	3½ cups
Baking powder	2 tsp.	1 Tbsp. + 1 tsp.
Baking soda	¼ tsp.	½ tsp.
Salt	½ tsp.	1 tsp.
Nutmeg	½ tsp.	1 tsp.
Mace	½ tsp.	1 tsp.

Melted shortening	¼ cup	½ cup
Eggs, well-beaten	2	4
Liquid low-calorie sweetener	2 Tbsp.	¼ cup
Vanilla	1 tsp.	2 tsp.
Bananas, mashed	2 medium	4 medium

Preheat oven to 350°F.

Sift flour, baking powder, soda, salt and spices.

Combine shortening, eggs, liquid sweetener and vanilla. Add to flour mixture; stir only to moisten. Fold in bananas.

Turn into a well-greased 7½x3¾x2½ inch loaf pan(s). Bake for 60 minutes.

Artichoke Heart with Vinegar, Oil and Basil

155 CALORIES/SERVING

Sliced Fresh Mushrooms

28 CALORIES/SERVING

Tuna-Filled Red and Green Peppers

260 CALORIES/SERVING

Anise Rye Toast

56 CALORIES/SERVING

Spiced Grapefruit and Orange Sections

52 CALORIES/SERVING

•

Fill the artichoke heart with a light oil and vinegar dressing flavored with fresh pepper and basil, and then circle with paper-thin mushroom slices.

Tuna Filled Red and Green Peppers can be made with shrimp or crab, or the stuffing can be baked on slices of fresh pineapple.

Thin-sliced rye, sparingly brushed with butter and then sprinkled with anise and toasted, is a low-calorie complement to many dishes—particularly seafood or fruit.

The Spiced Grapefruit and Orange dessert calls for ground ginger, but is even nicer when freshly grated or candied ginger is used; and whole cloves can replace the ground.

Total calories per person: 551.

TUNA-FILLED RED AND GREEN PEPPERS

260 CALORIES/SERVING
The entree is cooked, chilled and served at room temperature.

Ingredients	6 Portions	24 Portions
Onion, finely chopped	¾ cup	3 cups
Soy oil	2 Tbsp.	½ cup
Small tomatoes, peeled, seeded and chopped	6	24
Anchovies, rinsed and chopped	6	24
Capers	¼ cup + 2 Tbsp.	1½ cups
Currants	¼ cup + 2 Tbsp.	1½ cups
Pine nuts	¼ cup	1 cup
Tuna, packed in water, drained	3 cans (7 oz. ea.)	12 cans (7 oz. ea.)
Small sweet red peppers, tops cut off and seeded	6	24
Small green peppers, tops cut off and seeded	6	24
Salt	To taste	To taste
Pepper	To taste	To taste

Preheat oven to 350°F.

In a small skillet cook the onion in oil until tender. Add tomatoes and stir over moderate heat 8 to 10 minutes, until most of the liquid has evaporated. Stir in anchovies, capers, currants and pine nuts. Add tuna and season to taste with salt and pepper.

Mound the mixture into the peppers; place in lightly oiled baking dish and bake uncovered 35 minutes, or until the pepper shells are tender. Chill. Serve at room temperature.

SPICED GRAPEFRUIT AND ORANGE SECTIONS

52 CALORIES/SERVING
The spices turn simple citrus into something special.

Ingredients	6 Portions	24 Portions
Grapefruit sections	1½ cups	6 cups
Orange sections	1 cup	4 cups
Cinnamon stick	1	4
Ground cloves	¼ tsp.	1 tsp.
Ground ginger	¼ tsp.	1 tsp.

| Grated lemon peel | 1 Tbsp. | ¼ cup |
| Fresh mint sprig | 6 | 24 |

In saucepan combine grapefruit and orange sections, cinnamon stick, cloves, ginger, and lemon peel; simmer for 8 minutes.

Chill and serve in sherbet glasses. Garnish with sprig of mint.

Onion and Tomato-Stuffed Mushrooms
10 CALORIES/SERVING

Cold Lemon Chicken Breasts
246 CALORIES/SERVING

Dilled Vegetable Fingersticks
40 CALORIES/SERVING

Fresh Peach Yogurt Freeze
52 CALORIES/SERVING

•

The appetizer, Onion and Tomato Stuffed Mushrooms, is the only hot food served at this luncheon. If you prefer, you can change the order and serve the Dilled Vegetable Fingersticks as the appetizer and the mushrooms on the plate with the chicken breast.

Dilled Vegetable Fingersticks can be kept for as long as two weeks in the refrigerator, to have on hand for low-calorie nibbing.

Fresh Peach Yogurt Freeze is a breeze to put together if you have a blender or a food processor. Pop the peaches into boiling water to loosen the skin before peeling.

Total calories per person: 348.

ONION AND TOMATO-STUFFED MUSHROOMS

10 CALORIES/MUSHROOM

Heat them in your toaster oven or microwave to save energy.

Ingredients	6 Portions	24 Portions
Mushrooms, fresh	12 medium	48 medium
Tomatoes, chopped	½ cup	2 cups
Onions, green, chopped	1	4
Celery, chopped	¼ cup	1 cup
Dry mustard	¼ tsp.	1 tsp.
Fresh ground pepper	¼ tsp.	1 tsp.
Worcestershire sauce	⅛ tsp.	½ tsp.

Preheat oven to 375°F.

Wash mushrooms and hollow out stem side slightly. Chop the removed mushroom and stems with the tomato, green onion, and celery. Add spices and combine well.

Top each crown with some of the mixture. Bake a few minutes until hot.

COLD LEMON CHICKEN BREASTS

246 CALORIES/SERVING

The mayonnaise and cucumber spread gives each portion of wine-poached breast a special flavor.

Ingredients	6 Portions	24 Portions
Dry white wine	½ cup	2 cups
Water	1 cup	4 cups
Lemon juice and rind	¾ cup	3 cups
Boneless chicken breasts, split, skin removed	3	12
Mayonnaise	¼ cup	1 cup
Cucumber, peeled, seeded, finely chopped	¼ cup	1 cup
Marjoram	¼ tsp.	1 tsp.
Salt	¼ tsp.	1 tsp.
Pepper	¼ tsp.	1 tsp.
Lemon slices	6	24

In a saucepan combine wine, water and ½ cup (2 cups) lemon juice and rind. Bring to a boil. Add chicken. Cover. Cook over medium-low heat 20 minutes.

Remove chicken from broth. Set aside to cool.

Mix mayonnaise, cucumber, remaining lemon juice and rind, salt and pepper. Spread in a thin layer over chicken pieces. Top each with a lemon slice. Wrap in foil. Chill.

DILLED VEGETABLE FINGERSTICKS

40 CALORIES/½ CUP SERVING
You can't keep your fingers off of them.

Ingredients	8 Cups	24 Cups
Green beans	½ lb.	1½ lb.
Celery	½ lb.	1½ lb.
Green pepper	½ lb.	1½ lb.
Carrots	½ lb.	1½ lb.
Mustard seed	1 Tbsp.	3 Tbsp.
Dill weed, fresh	1 Tbsp.	3 Tbsp.
Garlic cloves	4	12
Water	2½ cups	7½ cups
Sugar	½ cup	1½ cups
Vinegar	1 cup	3 cups

Trim ends from green beans and wash thoroughly. Blanch by boiling in salted, rapidly boiling water until crisp-tender.

Cut celery and green pepper into thin strips and separately blanch; drain.

Peel carrots, cut into thin sticks and cook in boiling, salted water until crisp-tender; drain.

Combine vegetables; add dill weed, mustard seed and garlic cloves, halved.

In a saucepan combine water, sugar and vinegar; bring to a boil and pour over vegetables.

Cool; cover and chill overnight. Vegetables may be kept up to two weeks under refrigeration.

FRESH PEACH YOGURT FREEZE

52 CALORIES/¼ CUP SERVING
Yogurt, honey, fresh fruit and spices—what could be better?

Ingredients	6 Portions	24 Portions
Yogurt, plain	½ cup	2 cups
Fresh peaches, peeled and chopped	1½ cup	6 cups
Honey	3 Tbsp.	¾ cup
Lemon juice	½ Tbsp.	2 Tbsp.
Nutmeg	¼ tsp.	1 tsp.
Cinnamon	¼ tsp.	1 tsp.
Lemon rind, grated	½ tsp.	2 tsp.

Whirl all ingredients in blender until smooth. Pour into freezer trays until firm around the edges. Turn into a chilled bowl and beat until smooth. Return to tray and freeze until firm.

Let stand at room temperature to soften slightly before serving. Spoon into dessert glasses.

Melon Wedges with Prosciutto
110 CALORIES/SERVING

Tuna Yogurt Blend
212 CALORIES/SERVING

Red and Green Pepper Rings, Carrot and Celery Sticks, Raw Green Beans and Asparagus Spears
30 CALORIES/SERVING

Hard-Cooked Eggs
78 CALORIES/EGG

Warm Melba Toast
35 CALORIES/SERVING

Pineapple Crepes
135 CALORIES/SERVING

•

Wedges of low-calorie melon scantily clad with prosciutto make an excellent appetizer.

Make up individual servings, with each guest having a wine glass containing Tuna Yogurt Blend sitting on his plate, surrounded by vegetables. Melba toast adds a bit of substance without adding many calories.

The dessert is simply made, and you can top it with a warm pineapple sauce sparked with rum.

Total calories per person: 600.

TUNA YOGURT BLEND

212 CALORIES/SERVING

Brandy and mustard, plus anchovies and capers, add zip to this dip.

Ingredients	6 Portions	24 Portions
Tuna packed in water, drained	3 cans (3½ oz. ea.)	12 cans (3½ oz. ea.)
Anchovies, rinsed and chopped	1 can	4 cans
Capers	3 Tbsp.	¾ cup
Medium pitted ripe olives	15	60
Plain yogurt	½ cup	2 cups
Lemon juice	3 Tbsp.	¾ cup
Dijon-style mustard	1 tsp.	1 Tbsp. + 1 tsp.
Brandy	1½ tsp.	2 Tbsp.
Minced garlic	¼ tsp.	1 tsp.
Parsley, finely chopped	1 Tbsp.	¼ cup

In electric blender or food processor combine tuna, anchovies and capers; cover and process just until finely chopped. Add remainder of ingredients—except parsley—and blend.

Turn into small bowl, cover and refrigerate overnight. Serve sprinkled with parsley, as a dip or sauce with vegetables or eggs.

PINEAPPLE CREPES

135 CALORIES/SERVING

Pineapple, coconut and rum folded neatly inside low-calorie crepes.

Ingredients	6 Portions	24 Portions
Crushed unsweetened pineapple, packed in juice, drained	1 can (1 lb.)	4 cans (4 lb.)
Brown sugar (or artificial sweetener)	2 Tbsp.	½ cup
Lemon juice	To taste	To taste
Flaked coconut	⅓ cup	1⅓ cups
Rum	1 Tbsp.	¼ cup
Crepes (see Index)	6	24

Heat together the pineapple, sugar, lemon juice, coconut and rum. Serve folded inside crepes.

Sliced Tomatoes with Oregano
30 CALORIES/SERVING

Poached Halibut
135 CALORIES/3-OZ. SERVING

Neufchatel Brussels Sprouts
62 CALORIES/SERVING

Apple Cinnamon Cheesecake
251 CALORIES/SERVING

•

Poached halibut, garnished with greenery, is lovely to look upon, particularly if you're poaching a whole fish. When you're doing steaks, sprinkle them with a dash of paprika before serving.

Fresh brussels sprouts are much nicer than frozen—the frozen seem to become a little soggy when cooked. Mustard is the key ingredient in the sauce; vary it according to taste.

The Apple Cinnamon Cheesecake is flavored and sweetened with apple juice, and the cottage cheese contributes protein and minerals.

Total calories per person: 478.

POACHED HALIBUT

135 CALORIES/3-OZ. SERVING

It takes 5 minutes to make the stock and 10 to poach the fish.

Ingredients	6 Portions	24 Portions
Halibut	1½ lb.	6 lb.
Water	1¾ cups	7 cups
Salt	1 tsp.	1 Tbsp. + 1 tsp.
Lime juice	1 Tbsp.	¼ cup
Peppercorns	5	20
Onion, sliced	½	2
Bay leaf	2	8
Vinegar	1 tsp.	1 Tbsp. + 1 tsp.
Marjoram	⅛ tsp.	½ tsp.
Thyme	⅛ tsp.	½ tsp.

Simmer all ingredients except halibut for 5 minutes. Strain stock and pour over fish.

Simmer (do not boil) until fish has lost its translucency (about 10 to 15 minutes).

NEUFCHATEL BRUSSELS SPROUTS

62 CALORIES/SERVING

This low-calorie sauce has sliced water chestnuts for crunch.

Ingredients	8 Portions	24 Portions
Brussels sprouts, frozen or fresh	1 lb.	3 lb.
Water chestnuts, sliced	1 can (5 oz.)	3 cans (5 oz. ea.)
Neufchatel cheese	3 oz.	9 oz.
Skim milk	¼ cup	¾ cup
Prepared mustard	½ tsp.	1½ tsp.
Lemon juice	1 tsp.	1 Tbsp.
Nutmeg	¼ tsp.	¾ tsp.
White pepper	½ tsp.	1½ tsp.

Thaw brussels sprouts to separate (if frozen); divide larger sprouts in two and cook until crisp-tender; do not drain. Add sliced, drained water chestnuts to brussels sprouts.

Blend neufchatel cheese, skim milk, mustard, lemon juice, nutmeg and white pepper; beat well. Stir over low heat until hot.

Drain sprouts; pour sauce over them.

139

APPLE CINNAMON CHEESECAKE

251 CALORIES/SERVING

Walnut halves and apple slices flavored with rum or brandy top the luscious dessert.

Ingredients	6 Portions	24 Portions
Apple juice	¾ cup + 2 Tbsp.	3½ cups
Eggs, separated	1	4
Unflavored gelatin	1 envelope (1 Tbsp.)	4 envelopes (¼ cup)
Cold water	3 Tbsp.	¾ cup
Granulated sugar	¼ cup	1 cup
Low-fat creamed cottage cheese	1½ cups	6 cups
Ground cinnamon	1 tsp.	1 Tbsp. + 1 tsp.
Ground nutmeg	½ tsp.	2 tsp.
Mace	¼ tsp.	1 tsp.
Lemon rind	1 tsp.	1 Tbsp. + 1 tsp.

In a saucepan, mix the egg yolks and apple juice.

Sprinkle gelatin over cold water and let stand until water is absorbed. Add the sugar and gelatin to apple juice and heat until gelatin is dissolved, 3 to 4 minutes, stirring constantly. Set aside.

In a large bowl, beat the cottage cheese, cinnamon, nutmeg, mace and lemon rind until smooth and creamy. Gradually add the gelatin mixture, beat until well-blended. Chill in refrigerator or freezer until mixture begins to thicken.

In a large bowl, beat egg whites until peaks form. Carefully fold into the cheese mixture. Pour into springform pan. Chill at least 3 hours before serving.

When the cake is firm, spoon the Topping (recipe follows) over it, remove the springform from the sides and serve.

TOPPING

Ingredients	6 Portions	24 Portions
Red apples	1 medium	4 medium
Butter	1 Tbsp.	4 Tbsp.
Brown sugar	3 Tbsp.	¾ cup
Walnuts, chopped	¼ cup	1 cup
Rum or brandy	2 tsp.	2 Tbsp. + 2 tsp.

Cut apples into quarters. Remove core and cut into thin slices, leaving peel on. If the slices are large, cut them in halves.

In a frying pan, melt butter, add apple slices and sugar and cook until the apples are soft, but keep their shape.

Remove from heat and add nuts and rum or brandy. Let stand until juices are absorbed by the apples.

Asparagus Tips
and Tarragon Sour Cream
18 CALORIES/SERVING

Broiled Liver
110 CALORIES/3½-OZ. SERVING

Broiled Basil Tomatoes
45 CALORIES/SERVING

Brandied Coffee Jelly
with Custard Sauce
105 CALORIES/SERVING

•

Use tender new asparagus and serve the raw stalks with the tarragon-flavored dip either before or with lunch. The "sour cream" dip is a special low-cal brew.

Broiled Tomatoes are an English favorite served with every meal of the day including breakfast. They are low in calories and add a nice touch of color to any plate.

The Brandied Coffee Jelly with Custard Sauce is delightfully refreshing, summer or winter, and deliciously low in calories.

Total calories per person: 278.

ASPARAGUS TIPS AND TARRAGON SOUR CREAM

3 CALORIES/SPEAR   15 CALORIES/TABLESPOON OF SOUR CREAM
Cold asparagus with a tangy dip.

Ingredients	6 Portions	24 Portions
Skim milk	1/3 cup	1 1/3 cups
Lemon juice	1 tsp.	1 Tbsp. + 1 tsp.
Dry cottage cheese	1/2 lb.	2 lb.
Salt	1/4 tsp.	1 tsp.
Parsley	1/2 tsp.	2 tsp.
Tarragon	1 Tbsp.	1/4 cup
White pepper	1/8 tsp.	1/2 tsp.
Asparagus, ends trimmed, steamed and chilled		

Blend all ingredients except asparagus together in blender until smooth and creamy. Refrigerate until serving time. Serve dip with chilled asparagus.

BROILED BASIL TOMATOES

45 CALORIES/SERVING
Assemble ahead and broil at the last minute.

Ingredients	6 Portions	24 Portions
Soft bread crumbs	1/3 cup	1 1/3 cups
Minced onion	1 Tbsp.	1/4 cup
Tomatoes	3	12
Soy oil	3/4 Tbsp.	3 Tbsp.
Basil, fresh	1 Tbsp.	1/4 cup
Salt	1/2 tsp.	2 tsp.
Fresh ground black pepper	1/2 tsp.	2 tsp.
Watercress sprigs	6	24

Preheat oven to broil.

Combine bread crumbs, onion, oil, basil, salt and pepper and mix well.

Remove stem end from tomatoes, cut in half crosswise; spread crumb mixture over cut surfaces.

Broil crumb side up 5 to 6 inches from heat about 5 minutes or until golden brown.

Garnish with watercress.

143

BRANDIED COFFEE JELLY WITH CUSTARD SAUCE

105 CALORIES/SERVING (65 CALORIES/SERVING, PLAIN)

The brandy can be replaced with a chocolate-flavored liqueur for a mocha-flavored dessert.

Ingredients	8 Portions	24 Portions
Unflavored gelatin	**2 envelopes**	**6 envelopes**
Sugar	**½ cup**	**1½ cups**
Salt	**¼ tsp.**	**¾ tsp.**
Strong coffee	**3½ cups**	**10½ cups**
Brandy	**2 Tbsp.**	**6 Tbsp.**

Combine gelatin, sugar and salt in a saucepan. Stir in coffee. Place over low heat (about 200°F) and stir until gelatin is dissolved. Stir in brandy.

Pour into 9x5x2¾ inch loaf pan(s) and cool about 30 minutes. Chill until firm. Cut into ½ inch cubes. If desired, serve with *Custard Sauce* (recipe follows).

CUSTARD SAUCE

15 CALORIES/TABLESPOON

Ingredients	1½ Cups	4½ Cups
Liquid skim milk	**1½ cups**	**4½ cups**
Egg yolks	**2**	**6**
Sugar	**2 Tbsp.**	**⅓ cup**
Salt	**⅛ tsp.**	**¼ tsp.**
Vanilla extract	**¾ tsp.**	**2¼ tsp.**

Place milk in saucepan over low heat (about 200°F) until bubbles appear around the edges.

Beat egg yolks with a fork; blend in sugar and salt. Gradually stir about 1 cup of the hot milk into egg yolk mixture; return to saucepan. Cook over low heat, stirring constantly, until mixture coats a metal spoon.

Cool and add vanilla. Chill until serving time.

Marinated Brussels Sprouts
13 CALORIES/SERVING

Celery Fish Roll-Ups
123 CALORIES/SERVING

Carrots Cointreau
55 CALORIES/ONE-HALF CUP

Blueberry Ice
44 CALORIES/SERVING

•

Fresh or frozen brussels sprouts can be used in the Marinated Brussels Sprouts. When cooking frozen, be certain not to overcook; they're much better when served a bit crisp.

The Celery Fish Roll-Ups can be prepared with absolutely any fillet you can find. If you want to prepare this dish on a grill, just wrap the roll-ups in foil and bake over the coals.

Finishing carrots in a liqueur is a simple way of giving extra flavor. Precook the carrots; just before serving heat them in a very small amount of butter or margarine with a dash of Cointreau or any orange-flavored liqueur.

Blueberry Ice can be prepared from fresh or frozen berries—and they don't have to be blue.

Total calories per person: 235.

MARINATED BRUSSELS SPROUTS

An unusual appetizer, with only 13 calories per serving.

Ingredients	2 Cups	8 Cups
Brussels sprouts	2 cups	8 cups
Low-calorie Italian dressing, bottled	½ cup	2 cups
Garlic	1 clove	4 cloves
Onion, chopped	2 Tbsp.	½ cup
Parsley	1 Tbsp.	¼ cup
Dill weed	¼ tsp.	1 Tbsp. + 1 tsp.
Caraway seed	1 tsp.	1 Tbsp. + 1 tsp.
Sage	¼ tsp.	1 Tbsp.

Cut large sprouts in half. Cook in small amount of water until crisp-tender.

Combine Italian dressing, garlic, onion, parsley, dill weed, caraway and sage. Pour over warm brussels sprouts.

Cover, cool, and then marinate in refrigerator for several hours. Drain and serve with cocktail picks.

CELERY FISH ROLL-UPS

123 CALORIES/SERVING

Any kind of filleted fish can be prepared in this fashion.

Ingredients	6 Portions	24 Portions
Celery	1 stalk	4 stalks
Butter	1 Tbsp.	¼ cup
Onion, chopped	¼ cup	1 cup
Garlic, minced	1 clove	4 cloves
Tomatoes, chopped	½ lb.	2 lb.
Parsley, chopped	¼ cup	1 cup
Oregano	1 tsp.	1 Tbsp. + 1 tsp.
Salt	1¼ tsp.	1 Tbsp. + 2 tsp.
White pepper	⅛ tsp.	½ tsp.
Fish fillets	1½ lb.	6 lb.

Preheat oven to 350°F.

Trim tops from celery; separate celery into ribs; cut into ¼ inch thick slices; set aside.

In a saucepan melt butter and add onion and garlic; sauté 2 minutes. Add tomatoes, parsley, oregano, three-fourths of the salt, white pepper and reserved celery. Bring to boiling and remove from heat.

Spread half the celery mixture in a shallow casserole. Sprinkle fish with remaining salt. Spoon about 1 Tbsp. of celery mixture on each piece of fish; roll up and place in casserole; spoon remaining celery mixture over and around the fish.

Cover and bake until fish flakes easily when tested with a knife, approximately 20 minutes.

BLUEBERRY ICE

44 CALORIES/SERVING

There aren't many desserts that treat you so lightly.

Ingredients	8 Portions	24 Portions
Sugar	¼ cup	¾ cup
Unflavored gelatin	1½ tsp.	1 Tbsp. + 1½ tsp.
Water	1½ cups	4½ cups
Blueberries	1½ cups	4½ cups
Lemon juice	3 Tbsp.	½ cup + 1 Tbsp.
Fresh mint	8 pieces	24 pieces

In a saucepan combine sugar and gelatin; stir in two-thirds of the water. Heat and stir over medium heat until sugar and gelatin dissolve.

Remove from heat and add remaining water, berries and juice. Freeze in refrigerator tray until firm. Break into chunks and beat with electric mixer until smooth and creamy. Return to tray and freeze firm.

Divide into glass dessert cups and garnish with a sprig of mint.

Thin Italian Breadsticks
65 CALORIES/2 STICKS

Curried Tuna Custard
413 CALORIES/SERVING

Sliced Cucumbers with Coarse Salt
16 CALORIES/ONE-HALF CUCUMBER

Raspberry Granita
120 CALORIES/SERVING

Iced Tea with Lime and Mint

•

Breadsticks are low in calories and are satisfying to chew on before and during the meal.

Curried Tuna Custard is based upon low-calorie ricotta cheese and tuna packed in water (lower in calories than an oil pack). Serve it chilled with the sliced cucumbers.

Raspberry Granita is simply berries, orange juice, orange peel and a bit of the essence of raspberries found in the white alcohol Franboise. If you don't have Framboise, Kirsch or Fraise could be substituted.

Total calories per person: 614.

CURRIED TUNA CUSTARD

413 CALORIES/SERVING

A cold custard with tuna, peas and cheese making it colorful
and satisfying

Ingredients	6 Portions	24 Portions
Butter or margarine	2 Tbsp.	8 Tbsp.
Scallions, finely chopped	¾ cup	3 cups
Flour	¼ cup + 2 Tbsp.	1½ cups
Curry powder	1½ tsp.	2 Tbsp.
Skim milk	1½ cups	6 cups
Part skim milk ricotta cheese	2 cups	8 cups
Eggs	6	24
White pepper	½ Tbsp.	2 Tbsp.
Nutmeg	¼ tsp.	1 tsp.
Salt	1 Tbsp.	¼ cup
Tuna packed in water, drained	3 cans (7 oz. ea.)	12 cans (7 oz. ea.)
Frozen peas, thawed	1½ cups	6 cups
Lemon juice	1 Tbsp.	¼ cup

Preheat oven to 350°F.

In a small skillet melt butter, add scallions and cook until tender.
Blend in flour and curry powder; stir 2 minutes. Gradually stir in milk;
stir constantly until sauce thickens and comes to a boil.

In small bowl, beat ricotta, egg, salt, pepper and nutmeg. Stir in tuna,
curry sauce, peas and lemon juice.

Turn into 10-ounce ramekins or foil baking pans about 5 inches in diameter. Place in a pan of boiling water and bake 35 minutes, or until
custard is set.

Chill. Serve at room temperature.

RASPBERRY GRANITA

120 CALORIES/SERVING

Orange juice and peel complement any berry, as they do peaches and
apricots—try variations on this simple theme.

Ingredients	6 Portions	24 Portions
Grated peel and juice of oranges	1	4
Framboise liqueur	1 Tbsp.	¼ cup
Frozen raspberries	2 (10-oz.) pkg.	5 lb.

Chill individual sherbert dishes in refrigerator.

Cut frozen berries into large chunks.

Put orange juice, peel, and liqueur into blender or food processor. Puree, gradually adding raspberry chunks.

When all has been pureed, spoon immediately into chilled individual dishes and place in freezer.

Freeze for at least 3 hours. If the granita is frozen for more than 6 hours, remove from freezer 10 minutes before serving time.

Sliced Mushrooms and Bean Sprouts Sprinkled with Lemon Juice and Fresh Basil on Bibb Lettuce

35 CALORIES/SERVING

Eggs Baked in Tomato Shells

131 CALORIES/SERVING

Melba Toast

35 CALORIES/SERVING

Broccoli with Soy Nuts

40 CALORIES/½ CUP

Fresh Lemon Ice

130 CALORIES/SERVING

•

Eggs Baked in Tomato Shells are both colorful and nutritious. As you have the oven on, steam the broccoli by placing it in the oven on a tightly covered rack over boiling water. Serve sprinkled with soy nuts.

Lemon Ice should be served slightly soft like old-fashioned homemade ice cream. You won't want to serve the lemon ice in lemon shells with this menu (which already has tomato shells)—but you may wish to do so another time.

Total calories per person: 371.

EGGS BAKED IN TOMATO SHELLS

131 CALORIES/SERVING
Parmesan cheese and tarragon flavor this colorful dish.

Ingredients	6 Portions	24 Portions
Tomatoes	6 medium	24 medium
Salt	To taste	To taste
Tarragon leaves, chopped	¼ tsp.	1 tsp.
Ground black pepper	To taste	To taste
Eggs	6	24
Soft bread crumbs	3 Tbsp.	¾ cup
Parmesan cheese, grated	1 Tbsp.	¼ cup
Parsley, chopped	3 Tbsp.	¾ cup
Butter or margarine	1 tsp.	1½ tsp.

Preheat oven to 350°F.

Cut a thin slice from the stem end of each tomato. Run a paring knife around the inner rim of each tomato and carefully scoop out pulp. Sprinkle the inside of shells lightly with salt; invert on board to drain, about 10 minutes.

Combine tarragon, salt and pepper; blend well. Spoon about ½ teaspoon seasoning mixture into each shell. Break one egg into each shell.

Place on buttered baking pan in oven until eggs are beginning to set, about 8 minutes.

Combine bread crumbs, cheese and parsley. Sprinkle around outer edge of each tomato. Dot with butter. Place under preheated broiler until crumbs are lightly browned, 1 to 2 minutes.

FRESH LEMON ICE

130 CALORIES/SERVING
Banked on a bed of chipped ice, an assortment makes a magnificent display for a fancy buffet.

Ingredients	6 Portions	24 Portions
Sugar	1 cup	4 cups
Warm water	2 cups	9 cups
Unflavored gelatin, optional	2 tsp.	3 Tbsp.
Cold water, optional	2 Tbsp.	½ cup
Fresh lemon puree	¾ cup	3 cups + 2 Tbsp.

Stir sugar and water together in saucepan; heat to boiling and boil 5 minutes. Remove from heat.

If gelatin is used, sprinkle it over cold water to soften. Stir into hot syrup. Chill until cold.

To make puree, peel lemons, cutting away all white membrane (or use pulp scooped from lemons if you freeze ice in lemon shells). Cut into eighths, cut out white core and remove seeds. Puree in blender. Pour through coarse strainer to get out any white bits missed.

Mix puree with cold syrup. Pour into refrigerator trays and freeze until mushy.

In cold bowl with cold beaters, beat with electric mixer until frosty white and fluffy. Return quickly to refrigerator trays and freeze 3 to 4 hours.

LEMON ICE IN LEMON SHELLS: After lemon ice is beaten, freeze until it is moundable. Heap into large, scooped-out lemon shells. Freeze overnight. Remove from freezer 10 to 15 minutes before serving. Serve in coupe glasses lined with chipped ice, or on a star of shiny galax leaves.

Marinated Cucumber Salad
35 CALORIES/SERVING

Hot Cracked Crab in Dill Wine Sauce
252 CALORIES/SERVING

Green Rice
138 CALORIES/SERVING

Baked Coconut Bananas
104 CALORIES/SERVING

Zesty Orange Sauce
58 CALORIES/2 TABLESPOON SERVING

•

When you're not calorie-counting you can increase the butter content of the dill sauce, but even without butter it's excellent served hot with the chunks of crab.

Green Rice is a popular substitute for potatoes, and extremely nutritious.

Heat bananas only until warmed through, not until mushy. The well-spiced orange and lemon juice sauce is remarkably pleasant after the crab.

Total calories per person: 587.

MARINATED CUCUMBER SALAD

35 CALORIES/SERVING
Only 1 hour is needed for marinade to flavor the vegetables.

Ingredients	8 Portions	24 Portions
Cucumbers, sliced	3 cups	9 cups
Green peppers, sliced	1	3
Green onions, sliced	½ cup	1½ cups
Soy oil	2 Tbsp.	¼ cup + 2 Tbsp.
Lemon juice	2 Tbsp.	¼ cup + 2 Tbsp.
Vinegar	2 Tbsp.	¼ cup + 2 Tbsp.
Sugar	1 tsp.	1 Tbsp.
Dill weed	¼ tsp.	¾ tsp.
Mustard seed	¼ tsp.	¾ tsp.
White pepper	⅛ tsp.	¼ tsp.
Boston lettuce cups	8	24

In bowl combine cucumbers, green pepper and green onion. Blend together oil, lemon juice, vinegar, sugar, dill weed, mustard seed and white pepper.

Pour over vegetables and lightly toss. Cover and refrigerate 1 hour. Toss several times and serve in lettuce cups.

HOT CRACKED CRAB IN DILL WINE SAUCE

252 CALORIES/SERVING
At the Bankers Club in San Francisco they serve this dish with sour-dough bread for sauce dipping. (Bread has only 65 calories per ounce.)

Ingredients	6 Portions	24 Portions
Live crabs	24	96
Dry white wine		
Butter	3 Tbsp.	¾ cup
Garlic, crushed	1 clove	4 cloves
Fresh dill, minced	½ cup	2 cups

Preheat oven to 425°F.

Arrange crab upside down in roasting pan. Add ½-inch wine and sprinkle generously with lumps of butter mixed with garlic. Sprinkle with dill.

Bake 15 to 20 minutes or until done.

Crack the crab and serve hot in a deep dish with a generous amount of cooking sauce.

GREEN RICE

138 CALORIES/SERVING
Spinach, green pepper and green onions add the color.

Ingredients	6 Portions	24 Portions
Rice, washed, cooked and drained	1 cup, raw	4 cups, raw
American cheese, grated	3 Tbsp.	¾ cup
Green pepper, chopped	2 Tbsp.	½ cup
Green onions, chopped	2 Tbsp.	½ cup
Spinach, chopped	2 Tbsp.	½ cup
Eggs	1	4
Milk	1 cup	1 quart
Salt	To taste	To taste
Pepper	To taste	To taste

Preheat oven to 325°F.
Combine ingredients and bake in a well-greased baking pan for 45 minutes.

BAKED COCONUT BANANAS with ZESTY ORANGE SAUCE

104 CALORIES/SERVING
This dessert can be quickly done in the oven, a chafing dish or microwave—it's just a matter of heating the bananas.

Ingredients	6 Portions	24 Portions
Firm bananas	3	12
Butter, melted	1½ Tbsp.	¼ cup + 2 Tbsp.
Lemon peel, grated	½ tsp.	2 tsp.
Fresh lime juice	2 Tbsp.	½ cup
Unsweetened coconut	⅓ cup	1⅓ cups

Preheat oven to 375°F.
Grease baking dish.
Slice bananas thin and place in baking dish. Brush well with butter and sprinkle on grated lemon peel, lime juice and coconut.

Bake 15 minutes or until tender. Serve warm with *Zesty Orange Sauce* (recipe follows).

ZESTY ORANGE SAUCE

58 CALORIES/2 TABLESPOON SERVING

Ingredients	6 Portions	24 Portions
Sugar	¼ cup	1 cup
Cornstarch	1 Tbsp.	¼ cup
Salt	¼ tsp.	1 tsp.
Cinnamon	¼ tsp.	1 tsp.
Mace	¼ tsp.	1 tsp.
Nutmeg	¼ tsp.	1 tsp.
Boiling water	⅔ cup	2⅔ cups
Butter or margarine	2 Tbsp.	8 Tbsp.
Orange peel, grated	1 Tbsp.	¼ cup
Fresh orange juice	¼ cup	1 cup
Fresh lemon juice	1 Tbsp.	¼ cup

In saucepan combine sugar, cornstarch, salt, cinnamon, mace and nutmeg. Gradually stir in boiling water; bring water to a boil again.

Cook, stirring constantly, until thickened, about 5 minutes. Then stir in butter, orange peel, orange and lemon juices.

Serve warm over *Baked Coconut Bananas*.

157

FOUR
Seasonal Favorites

I remember standing on an airstrip in Tahiti (in December) and watching a crew load crates of tropical fruit aboard our plane. It didn't seem strange in Tahiti, but it certainly did when I walked down a snowy New York street the next day and saw tropical fruits for sale (at astronomical prices).

Food is still, to a large extent, seasonal wherever you may live. Tomatoes and strawberries, possible exceptions, have a recognizable shape and color year-round, but certainly don't have the flavor in the winter that they do in season.

Seasons should have a bearing on menu planning, it makes sense to concentrate on foods when they are at their peak of flavor and freshness and about as inexpensive as they ever will be.

Tradition also plays a part in seasonal favorites. I'm entirely certain that rhubarb pie would not taste half as good for Thanksgiving as pumpkin pie does.

Avocado Half with Sour Cream and Red Caviar

Broiled Rock Lobster Tails with Rosy Butter and Green Mayonnaise

Garden Vegetable Salad

Crescent Rolls

Pineapple Yogurt Sherbet

Cookies

•

Half an avocado makes an excellent, but filling, appetizer. Leave the meat in the skin and fill the cavity with sour cream, then sprinkle with red caviar.

Broiled Rock Lobster Tails are most impressive served piggyback. Melted butter is the most frequent companion for lobster; the Rosy Butter is an interesting variation. If you have the time, it is even nicer to serve a Green Mayonnaise.

Garden Vegetable Salad makes a light accompaniment for the rich lobster—allow 30 minutes' chilling time when you're preparing it.

BROILED ROCK LOBSTER TAILS

The lobster appears to be riding atop its own shell.

Thaw South African rock lobster tails. Insert point of kitchen shears between meat and hard shell on back. Clip hard shell down the center, leaving tail "fan" intact. Do not remove underside membrane.

Gently open shell, separating it from meat. Lift raw tail meat through split shell to rest on outside of shell, leaving meat attached to fan end of shell.

Preheat broiler and arrange shells, with meat "piggybacked" on top, in shallow broiler pan. Brush with melted butter (or any desired sauce) and broil about 4 inches from heat.

Serve with *Rosy Butter* and *Green Mayonnaise* (recipes follow).

TIMETABLE FOR BROILING SOUTH AFRICAN ROCK LOBSTER TAILS ONLY
(in minutes)

2 oz.	3 oz.	4 oz.	5 oz.	6 oz.	7 oz.	8 oz.
6	8	10	12	14	16	18

ROSY BUTTER

A sauce well-suited to any broiled seafood.

Ingredients	¾ Cup	3 Cups
Butter or margarine	½ cup (1 stick)	2 cups (1 lb.)
Catsup	¼ cup	1 cup
Lemon juice	1 Tbsp.	¼ cup
Tabasco sauce	Dash	¼ tsp.

In a small saucepan combine all ingredients and stir until smooth and melted.

Serve warm.

GREEN MAYONNAISE

A tangy accent for seafoods.

Ingredients	2 Cups	8 Cups
Mayonnaise	1½ cups	6 cups
Watercress, chopped	¾ cup	3 cups
Parsley, chopped	¼ cup	1 cup
Chives, chopped	2 Tbsp.	½ cup
Prepared mustard	2 tsp.	2 Tbsp. + 2 tsp.

162

| Lemon juice | 2 Tbsp. | ½ cup |
| Salt | To taste | To taste |

Combine all ingredients except salt in a blender. Whirl until smooth. Season to taste with salt.

Serve warm or cold.

GARDEN VEGETABLE SALAD

Honey and vinegar dress steamed vegetables.

Ingredients	4 Portions	24 Portions
Fresh asparagus, sliced diagonally, about 2 inches long	1 cup	6 cups
Fresh green beans, sliced diagonally, about 2 inches long	1 cup	6 cups
Fresh or thawed frozen peas	1 cup	6 cups
DRESSING		
Cider vinegar	2 Tbsp.	¾ cup
Honey	2 tsp.	¼ cup
Garlic salt	1 tsp.	2 Tbsp.
Pepper	¼ tsp.	1½ tsp.
Radishes, sliced	1 cup	6 cups
Marinated artichoke hearts	1 jar (6 oz.)	6 jars (6 oz. ea.)

Arrange asparagus, beans and peas (do not cook thawed peas) in a vegetable steamer and steam over boiling water just until barely tender when pierced, about 2 to 4 minutes.

Plunge vegetables in cold water to cool quickly; drain well. Cover and refrigerate if cooked ahead.

In a bowl or jar, combine vinegar, honey, garlic salt, and pepper. Drain marinade from artichoke hearts into vinegar mixture; stir or shake together.

Pour dressing over vegetables; add radishes and marinated artichoke hearts; toss, cover and chill about 30 minutes.

PINEAPPLE YOGURT SHERBET

Make at least a day ahead so that it can mellow.

Ingredients	1 Quart	1 Gallon
Crushed pineapple	1 can (8¼ oz.)	4 cans (8¼ oz. ea.)
Unflavored gelatin	1½ tsp.	2 Tbsp.
Sugar	¾ cup	3 cups
Salt	⅛ tsp.	½ tsp.
Yogurt, plain	1 container (16 oz.)	4 lb.
Lemon juice	1 tsp.	1 Tbsp. + 1 tsp.
Lemon peel, grated	1 tsp.	1 Tbsp. + 1 tsp.
Vanilla extract	½ tsp.	2 tsp.
Angostura bitters	1 tsp.	1 Tbsp.
Egg white	1	4

Turn pineapple into small saucepan, and sprinkle with gelatin. Let stand 5 minutes. Place over low heat, and stir until gelatin dissolves. Remove from heat.

Set aside 2 Tbsp. (½ cup) sugar for egg white. Stir remaining sugar and salt into pineapple. Cool to room temperature.

Stir in yogurt, lemon juice and peel, and vanilla. Turn into loaf pan(s). Freeze until firm.

When mixture is frozen, beat egg white to soft peaks. Beat in reserved sugar, a little at a time, making a meringue.

Turn sherbet into large chilled bowl, and beat at low speed until smooth. Increase speed and beat until fluffy. Fold in meringue.

Return sherbet to pan and freeze firm. Cover.

Deep-Fried Bacon-Wrapped Oysters
Beef Salad Vinaigrette
Fresh Berries with
Crème Fraîche

•

Oysters aren't unusual; fried oysters aren't unusual; bacon-wrapped oysters aren't unusual—but deep fried bacon-wrapped oysters are. The idea is from a private club where they ran out of chicken livers one day and substituted oysters—the result was considered to be ambrosia.

The beef salad can be made from boiled or roast beef. If you don't have ready access to cornichons use any sour pickle available.

Crème Fraîche, the thick cream with the slightly nutty flavor (some call it "just turning sour" flavor), beloved by the French, costs a great deal—when you can find it. A suitable substance can be hand-fabricated at home, and it does go nicely with any fruit.

DEEP-FRIED BACON-WRAPPED OYSTERS

A most unusual way of bringing oysters out of their shell.

Ingredients	6 Portions	24 Portions
Oysters	24	96
Bacon, sliced, cut in half	12 slices	48 slices
Egg, beaten	1	4
Milk	1 Tbsp.	¼ cup
Fine bread crumbs	1½ cups	6 cups
Soy oil for deep frying	As needed	As needed

Wrap each oyster in half slice of bacon and fasten with a toothpick. Combine egg and milk; dip oyster in egg mixture. Roll oyster in bread crumbs; shake off excess. Deep fry at 375°F until golden brown.

Remove toothpick if served as an appetizer; leave toothpick if served as an hors d'oeuvre. (The breaded uncooked oysters may be kept in the freezer until needed.)

BEEF SALAD VINAIGRETTE

Julienne strips of beef in a tangy mustard dressing.

Ingredients	6 Portions	24 Portions
SALAD		
Freshly cooked beef cut into julienne strips	4 cups	16 cups
Celery	2 stalks	8 stalks
Onion, preferably red	1	4
Tomatoes	2 medium (about ½ lb.)	8 medium (about 2 lb.)
Cornichons (imported sour gherkins)	4	16
Garlic, finely minced	1 clove	3 cloves
Parsley, finely chopped	2 Tbsp.	½ cup
SAUCE		
Mustard, preferbaly Dijon	1 Tbsp.	¼ cup
Red wine vinegar	2 Tbsp.	½ cup
Salt	To taste	To taste
Pepper, freshly ground	To taste	To taste
Soy oil, chilled	⅔ cup	2⅔ cups

Place meat in a mixing bowl. Trim celery; cut into 1-inch lengths. Cut each length into very fine matchlike strips (julienne).

Peel onion(s), cut in half and slice each half as thinly as possible. There should be slightly less than 1 cup (4 cups).

Peel and core tomatoes. Cut in half and squeeze each half gently to extract the seeds. Cut each half into small cubes. There should be about 1 cup (4 cups).

Trim off ends of the cornichons. Cut cornichons into fine matchlike strips (julienne). There should be about ⅓ cup (1⅓ cups).

Add celery, onion(s), tomatoes, cornichons, garlic and parsley to meat.

Place mustard, vinegar, salt and pepper in a cold mixing bowl. Gradually add the oil, stirring rapidly with a whisk.

Pour it over the beef. Toss to blend. Serve at room temperature or slightly lukewarm.

CRÈME FRAÎCHE

The cream thickens and takes on a nutty flavor, but it is not sour. It should keep about 10 days under refrigeration and is delicious on fruits and desserts where you might ordinarily use whipped cream.

Ingredients	1 Cup	4 Cups
Heavy cream	1 cup	1 quart
Buttermilk	1 tsp.	1 Tbsp. + 1 tsp.

Stir buttermilk into cream and heat to lukewarm (not over 135°F).

Pour mixture into loosely covered jar and let stand at room temperature until it has thickened. This will take 5 to 8 hours on a hot day, 24 to 36 when the temperature is cooler.

Stir, cover and refrigerate.

Herbed Olives
Scampi à la James
Parslied Rice
Green Peas with Mint
Hard Rolls
Nockerln in Lemon Sauce

•

Herbed Olives are quickly made from green olives stuffed with pimiento or almonds, but must be marinated several hours for the flavors to blend. Keep the marinade and add olives on a regular basis.

The Scampi à la James recipe comes from the Executive Club in Jacksonville, Florida, where they like their shrimp flavored with garlic and hot red pepper.

Nockerln in Lemon Sauce is an elegant, light dessert from Salzburg, Austria. It must be served as soon as it's cooked. The Lemon Sauce can be prepared in advance. The Nockerln can be served with fresh fruits, if desired.

HERBED OLIVES

Several hours marination time needed, for the herb flavors
to be absorbed.

Ingredients	6 Portions	24 Portions
Stuffed green olives	18	72
Wine vinegar	1 Tbsp.	¼ cup
Oregano	¼ tsp.	1 tsp.
Thyme	Pinch	⅛ tsp.
Fennel	Pinch	⅛ tsp.
Olive oil	As needed	As needed

Drain half of the brine from the olives in the jar or can and add
vinegar and herbs to remaining brine and olives.

Fill jar with olive oil and marinate several hours.

Save the marinade for future olive storage or for use in salad dressings.

SCAMPI À LA JAMES

The shrimp can be prepared at tableside in an electric wok.

Ingredients	6 Portions	24 Portions
Butter	6 Tbsp.	¾ lb.
Olive oil	¾ cup	3 cups
Hot red peppers, split and seeded	3	12
Garlic cloves, finely chopped	3	12
Shrimp, fresh, peeled and veined, tail on	3 lb.	12 lb.
Capers	3 Tbsp.	¾ cup
Parsley, finely chopped	3 Tbsp.	¾ cup
Oregano	1½ tsp.	2 Tbsp.
Salt	To taste	To taste
Pepper	To taste	To taste

Melt butter, add olive oil, bring to high temperature. Drop in hot
peppers and cook 1 minute.

Remove peppers, sauté garlic 2 minutes and add shrimp. Brown
shrimp on each side. Add capers and parsley; cook 2 more minutes.

Sprinkle with oregano, salt and pepper; stir together and serve in
scallop shells.

NOCKERLN IN LEMON SAUCE

Sweet, meringue-like dumplings floating on a lemon sauce.

Ingredients	6 Portions	24 Portions
LEMON SAUCE		
Butter or margarine	4 Tbsp.	1 cup
Sugar	½ cup	2 cups
Cornstarch	2 tsp.	2 Tbsp. + 2 tsp.
Lemon juice	¼ cup	1 cup
Grated lemon peel	½ tsp.	2 tsp.
SOUFFLÉ		
Eggs	4	16
Salt	⅛ tsp.	½ rounded tsp.
Cream of tartar	⅛ tsp.	½ rounded tsp.
Sugar	⅓ cup	1⅓ cups
Flour	2 Tbsp.	½ cup
Grated lemon peel	1 tsp.	1 Tbsp. + 1 tsp.
Small strawberries, sliced, optional	1 cup	4 cups
Confectioners' sugar	As needed	As needed

Melt butter or margarine.

Combine sugar and cornstarch; stir into melted butter. Gradually add lemon juice and grated lemon peel. Cook, stirring until sauce boils and thickens; set aside.

Preheat oven to 350°F.

Separate eggs, placing whites in large mixing bowl and yolks in smaller bowl. Beat egg whites with salt and cream of tartar until stiff peaks form. Gradually beat in sugar, beating until whites are very stiff and shiny; set aside.

Using the same beaters, beat yolks until lemon colored; add flour and grated lemon peel. Continue beating until yolks are thickened; gently fold yolks into beaten whites.

Pour prepared lemon sauce into a baking dish and spoon soufflé mixture in mounds (1 per serving) over sauce.

Bake soufflé in center of oven for 12 to 15 minutes. Remove from oven, dust with confectioners' sugar, and serve, spooning lemon sauce over each serving.

Garnish with strawberries or other fresh fruit, if desired.

Apple Cider
Potato Pancakes
Thick Slices of Slab Bacon or Ham, Broiled
Hot Cranberry Sauce with Cinnamon
Buttermilk Biscuits
Fudge Sauced Ice Cream Pie

•

The Apple Cider could be mulled with cloves and cinnamon and served hot by the fire while guests gather.

The ingredients for the Potato Pancakes can be done ahead if you use ascorbic acid (available in grocery and drug stores) to help prevent discoloration of the shredded potatoes.

Hot Cranberry Sauce can be made from fresh berries, or the canned whole berry sauce can be heated and served.

The shell of the ice cream pie is made from any kind of chocolate cookie crumbs. The shell can be filled with your choice of ice cream—coffee, peppermint, and pistachio are special favorites.

POTATO PANCAKES

Also delicious served with roast pork or sausages of any kind
and applesauce.

Ingredients	6 Portions	24 Portions
Potatoes, peeled	5 medium	20 medium
Ascorbic acid powder, optional	1 tsp.	1 Tbsp.
Onion, grated, optional	1 Tbsp.	¼ cup
Eggs, slightly beaten	3	12
Flour	2 Tbsp.	½ cup
Salt	1 tsp.	1 Tbsp. + 1 tsp.
Pepper, freshly ground	To taste	To taste
Baking powder	¼ tsp.	1 tsp.
Soy oil for frying		

Shred potatoes on a fine shredder to make about 3 cups (12 cups).
Add ascorbic acid mixture to potatoes as you grate them, stirring to in-
corporate more as needed. Blend potatoes with onion and eggs.

Mix together flour, salt, pepper and baking powder; blend into potato mixture.

Pour oil to a depth of about ⅛ inch in a heavy frying pan and heat
until very hot. Using about ⅓ cup of batter per cake, drop into hot fat
and brown both sides, turning only once.

Serve crisp and hot. Cakes may be kept warm in an oven by placing
on baking sheets lined with paper towels. Cover with aluminum foil
punched with holes to release steam.

FUDGE SAUCED ICE CREAM PIE

A chocolate cookie crust holds ice cream indefinitely in the freezer.
Serve with chocolate sauce, and to splurge top the sauce with
whipped cream flavored with green Creme de Menthe.

Ingredients	1 Pie	4 Pies
SHELL		
Chocolate cookie crumbs	1¼ cups	5 cups
Butter or margarine, softened	¼ cup	1 cup
FILLING		
Ice cream, softened	3 pints	3 quarts
SAUCE		
Butter or margarine	¼ cup	1 cup
Milk	½ cup	2 cups
Semi-sweet chocolate	6 oz.	24 oz.

| **Rum or Creme de Cacao,** | | |
| **optional** | **1 tsp.** | **1 Tbsp.** |

Blend chocolate cookie crumbs with soft butter and pack against bottom of pie plate(s). Chill 1 hour.

Fill with ice cream and freeze until firm.

Combine sauce ingredients in saucepan and heat to melt chocolate. Blend until smooth and stir in Rum or Creme de Cacao.

Serve sauce warm or at room temperature.

Pickled Herring

Marinated Salmon with
Mustard-Dill Sauce

Raw Vegetable Medley

Pumpernickel Bread

Crepes Spitzbergen

•

The Mustard-Dill Sauce complements almost any fish or
vegetable dish. You could even skip making a dressing for the
raw vegetables and use the Mustard-Dill Sauce only, if you
wanted to save time. The light dressings are a nice change from
the heavier dips often served with raw vegetables.

Crepes, filled with ice cream and strawberries, are the basis for
the dessert, but it's hard to find them under the meringue
cover. A Flaming Strawberry Sauce makes it even more
spectacular.

MARINATED SALMON

Mackerel, trout, salmon trout and char (brook trout) can be prepared in this same way.

Ingredients	3 Portions	24 Portions
Salmon	1 lb.	8 lb.
Salt	2 Tbsp.	1 cup
Sugar	2 Tbsp.	1 cup
Saltpeter	Pinch	½ tsp.
White peppercorns, crushed	5	40
Dill, or spruce twigs	As needed	As needed

Salmon are best for marinating in the spring. If possible, select a middle cut. Scrape the salmon and dry it thoroughly with a cloth, but do not rinse the fish. Slit the salmon open along the backbone and take it out, also pull out any small bones.

Mix the salt, sugar and saltpeter and rub the mixture into the salmon. Put a layer of dill or spruce twigs (if available) into a shallow dish.

Put one half of the salmon on top with the skin side downwards. Sprinkle the fish with plenty of dill together with the crushed peppercorns. Put the other half of the salmon on top with the skin side uppermost. Cover the salmon with dill or spruce twigs.

Put a weighted chopping board or dish on top of the salmon and leave in a cool, dark place for 48 hours.

The salmon is then ready to serve but can be stored for a week in the refrigerator.

MUSTARD-DILL SAUCE

Excellent served with fish aspic, baked fish, cold vegetables and salads.

Ingredients	4 Portions	24 Portions
Egg yolk, hard-cooked	1	6
Egg yolk, raw	1	6
Vinegar or lemon juice	1 to 1½ Tbsp.	6 to 9 Tbsp.
Mustard, French	1 tsp.	2 Tbsp.
Salt	1 tsp.	2 Tbsp.
White pepper or paprika	⅛ tsp.	¾ tsp.
Sugar	1 tsp.	2 Tbsp.
Soy oil	1 cup	6 cups
Heavy cream, whipped	½ cup + 2 Tbsp.	3⅓ cups
Dill, chopped	2 Tbsp.	¾ cup

This sauce may be made with or without oil.

Mash the cold, cooked egg yolk in a bowl and mix it with the raw egg yolk. Sieve the mixture if it is granular. Mix the yolks with vinegar or lemon juice, mustard, salt, seasoning and sugar. Add the oil, beating vigorously, first a drop at a time, increasing to a trickle. If the sauce curdles, carefully fold in a little unbeaten heavy cream.

Fold in the cream carefully. Add the dill and taste the sauce for seasoning.

RAW VEGETABLE MEDLEY

Serve with fried meat, fish dishes or as a separate course.

Ingredients	4 Portions	24 Portions
Fennel, savoy or celery cabbage	8 oz.	3 lb.
Beets, coarsely grated	¼ cup	1½ cups
Carrot, coarsely grated	1	6
or	or	or
Brussels sprouts	½ cup	3 cups
or	or	or
White cabbage, shredded	½ cup	3 cups
Apple, coarsely grated	1	6
Leek, sliced	1	6

Arrange the vegetables in groups and serve them with one of the salad dressings (recipes follow). Alternatively, mix the vegetables with the dressing in a bowl.

DRESSINGS

Ingredients	4 Portions	24 Portions
LEMON DRESSING		
Lemon juice	2 Tbsp.	¾ cup
Soy oil or water, or half quantity of each	⅓ cup	2 cups
Sugar	To taste	To taste
ONION AND PAPRIKA DRESSING		
Onion juice or grated onion	2 tsp.	¼ cup
Paprika	¼ tsp.	1½ tsp.
Mustard, dry	¼ tsp.	1½ tsp.
Sugar	½ tsp.	1 Tbsp.

Mix the ingredients by shaking or whisking them together. Taste for seasoning.

CREPES SPITZBERGEN

The Scandinavian version of strawberry crepes.

Ingredients	6 Portions	24 Portions
CREPES AND FILLING		
Eggs, separated	4	16
Sugar	1 Tbsp.	¼ cup
Flour, sifted	1 cup	4 cups
Milk	1½ cups	6 cups
Beer	1½ cups	6 cups
Lemon rind, grated	1 lemon	4 lemons
Butter, melted	2 Tbsp.	½ cup
Salt	Pinch	¼ tsp.
Vanilla ice cream	1 pint	2 quarts
Strawberries, sliced	1 cup	4 cups
MERINGUE		
Egg whites	2	8
Sugar, granulated	2 Tbsp.	½ cup
FLAMING SAUCE		
Strawberries, to make	1 cup puree	4 cups puree
Orange juice, undiluted frozen concentrate	2 Tbsp.	½ cup
Currant jelly	1 Tbsp.	¼ cup
Brandy	2 Tbsp.	½ cup
Orange-flavored liqueur	3 Tbsp.	¾ cup

CREPES: Combine egg yolks and sugar and stir until sugar is dissolved. Add flour alternately with milk and beer, beating well after each addition. Stir in lemon rind, melted butter and salt. Beat egg whites until stiff and fold into batter. Cook crepes on 8-inch skillet, using 3 Tbsp. of batter for each crepe. Cool.

MERINGUE: Beat egg whites until stiff. Beat in sugar.

Spoon ice cream and strawberries onto crepes. Roll once and cover with meringue. Slip under broiler to brown quickly.

SAUCE: Bring puree, juice concentrate and jelly to simmering temperature. In a separate pan combine the brandy and liqueur and warm slightly. Pour the strawberry puree over the browned crepes.

Ignite the heated brandy and liqueur and pour the blazing spirits over all.

Lobster Potato Salad

Sliced Tomatoes, Cucumbers and Yellow Squash
Sprinkled with Fresh Dill

Eight-Layer Blueberry Cake

•

The hearty salad can be served in individual portions with rock lobster shells used as garnish or it can be made in one large bowl for a buffet.

Each thin layer of the Blueberry Cake is baked separately, and cooled. The cake is assembled with orange-flavored liqueur added to the whipped cream that is spread between layers.

LOBSTER POTATO SALAD

The most elegant, and the best, potato salad ever to grace
a summer table.

Ingredients	8 Portions	24 Portions
Rock lobster tails, frozen	¾ lb.	4 to 5 lb.
Potatoes	3 lb.	9 lb.
Onion, diced	⅓ cup	1 cup
Celery, diced	1 cup	3 cups
Salt	1½ tsp.	2 Tbsp.
White pepper	½ tsp.	1½ tsp.
Mayonnaise	2 cups	6 cups
Sour cream	½ cup	1½ cups
Heavy cream	½ cup	1½ cups
Bacon, cooked crisp, crumbled	6 slices	18 slices
Eggs, hard-cooked, sieved	2	6

Drop frozen rock lobster tails into boiling salted water. When water
reboils, cook for 2 to 3 minutes. Drain immediately and drench with
cold water. With scissors cut away underside membrane and pull out
meat in one piece. Dice. Chill.

Peel and boil potatoes. Drain and dice while still warm. Mix potatoes
with onion, celery, salt, pepper, mayonnaise and creams. Fold in rock
lobster pieces.

Spoon salad into a bowl or individual plates lined with lettuce leaves.
Sprinkle top with crumbled bacon and sieved eggs. Chill thoroughly
before serving.

EIGHT-LAYER BLUEBERRY CAKE

An imposing finale for any meal.

Ingredients	1 Cake (12 Servings)	2 Cakes (24 Servings)
Eggs	4	8
Sugar	1 cup	2 cups
Water	½ cup	1 cup
Vanilla extract	1 tsp.	2 tsp.
Sifted all-purpose flour	1 cup	2 cups
Baking powder	2 tsp.	4 tsp.
Fresh blueberries, rinsed and drained	2 cups	4 cups
Heavy cream, whipped	2 cups	1 quart
Confectioners' sugar	⅓ cup	⅔ cup
Orange-flavored liqueur	2 Tbsp. (1 oz.)	¼ cup (2 oz.)

Preheat oven to 375°F.

Beat eggs until thick and lemon colored. Gradually beat in sugar and whip until very thick. Stir in water and vanilla. Fold in flour and baking powder.

Line an 8-inch layer cake pan with foil. Grease foil and spoon in ¾ cup of the batter. Sprinkle ¼ cup of the blueberries over the batter.

Bake for 12 minutes or until edge is lightly browned. Loosen edges with a knife and turn out on a rack. Carefully strip off foil. Cool. Repeat until you have 8 layers.

Beat cream with sugar until stiff. Fold in liqueur. Spread cream between cake layers. Garnish cake with extra blueberries. (Cut cake with serrated-edged knife.)

Bread Sticks
Medallions of Veal with Lemon Butter
Tomatoes Sicilian Style
Spinach Noodles with Pine Nuts
Marinated Fresh Fruit
Lemon Ice

•

This is a very filling lunch; for guests with smaller appetites, eliminate the spinach noodles with Pine Nuts and serve a half-portion of the Tomatoes Sicilian Style to each person.

Bread sticks can serve to keep appetites under control while final preparation takes place in the kitchen, and then go on to accompany the meal, if desired.

If time doesn't permit preparation of the fruit, serve cookies with the Lemon Ice and pour a little Strega or Galliano over top.

MEDALLIONS OF VEAL with LEMON BUTTER

Lemon adds piquancy to thinly sliced veal.

Ingredients	6 Portions	24 Portions
Veal scallops	1½ lb.	6 lb.
Flour	¼ cup + 2 Tbsp.	1½ cups
Salt	To taste	To taste
Freshly ground black pepper	To taste	To taste
Eggs (beaten)	5	18
Milk	3 Tbsp.	¾ cup
Olive oil	3 Tbsp.	¾ cup
Butter	3 Tbsp.	1½ sticks
Lemon juice	3 Tbsp.	¾ cup
Fresh chopped parsley (optional)	3 Tbsp.	¾ cup
Thin slices lemon (garnish)	18	72

Trim and flatten veal scallops. Mix flour, salt and pepper. Dredge veal in seasoned flour.

Beat and mix eggs and milk. Dredge floured veal in egg mixture.

Heat oil in a large skillet until it sizzles. Sauté veal on both sides until golden brown, quickly. Remove veal from skillet and place on hot plate. Discard oil.

Heat butter and lemon juice in skillet and add cooked veal, stirring and coating well with sauce. Just before removing veal, sprinkle with chopped parsley if desired.

Remove veal from skillet and arrange on hot plate. Pour a little of the sauce over veal and garnish with lemon slices.

TOMATOES SICILIAN STYLE

Anchovy fillets, capers, olives and bread crumbs stuff baked tomato halves.

Ingredients	4 Portions	24 Portions
Small firm tomatoes	4	24
Olive oil	⅓ cup	2 cups
Onion, finely chopped	1 small	6 small
Pitted black olives	8	48
Anchovy fillets, finely chopped	4	24
Fresh parsley, chopped fine	1 Tbsp.	⅓ cup
Capers	1 Tbsp.	⅓ cup
White wine	1 Tbsp.	⅓ cup
Bread crumbs, optional	¼ cup	1½ cups

| Salt | To taste | To taste |
| White pepper | To taste | To taste |

Preheat oven to 350°F.

Cut tomatoes horizontally and scoop out some of the pulp from the center, leaving a large wall. Wash tomato, removing all the seeds and pulp; chop pulp medium.

Heat oil in a small saucepan and cook onions for several minutes (do not brown). Save some black olives for garnishing and chop the remainder medium dice.

Mix olives, anchovies, parsley, capers, white wine, bread crumbs, salt and pepper; add onion mixture and mix well.

Stuff tomatoes with mixture; garnish with black olive halves. Arrange stuffed tomatoes in an oiled shallow baking dish; bake for 30 minutes.

MARINATED FRESH FRUIT

Top with a sprig of mint or unsweetened whipped cream.

Ingredients	6 Portions	24 Portions
Oranges (peeled and cut into segments)	2	8
Grapefruit	1	4
Peaches (peeled and sliced)	2	8
Pear (peeled and sliced)	1	4
Strega liqueur		
Lemon Ice (see index)	6 scoops	24 scoops

Peel and cut all fruit and marinate in the Strega for at least ½ hour. Scoop lemon ice into a glass.

Spoon marinated fruit over the *Lemon Ice.*

Egg Rolls with Mustard Sauce
Watercress Soup
Stuffed Sea Bass
Fried Rice
Stir-Fried Mushrooms
Chilled Lichi with Tiffin Liqueur or Plum Wine

•

Good Egg Rolls can be found in freezer cases at supermarkets and they're an easy finger food to enjoy while guests gather. Use powdered mustard and cider vinegar to make a tangy mustard dipping sauce.

One of the Sea Bass stuffing ingredients, Chinese sausages, almost has to be secured at a Chinese grocery store—though you can trade authenticity for expediency and use a spicy link sausage.

Fried Rice can be made ahead, packed in small cups or bowls and reheated in a microwave, or, put the molds in a pan of hot water, cover with foil and reheat in the oven while the fish bakes.

WATERCRESS SOUP

Simply made but very nutritious.

Ingredients	6 Portions	24 Portions
Chicken broth, canned or homemade	3½ cups	14 cups
Soy sauce	2 tsp.	3 Tbsp.
Fresh ginger root, sliced	2 to 4 slices	15 slices
Water	½ cup	2 cups
Watercress (without stems)	1 bunch	4 bunches
Green onions, finely sliced	2 Tbsp.	½ cups
Salt	To taste	To taste
Sugar	To taste	To taste

Combine chicken broth, soy sauce, ginger root and water. Simmer 15 minutes.

Add watercress and green onions. Cover and simmer 2 minutes. Season to taste and serve at once.

STUFFED SEA BASS

The stuffing is Chinese sausages, scallops and water chestnuts.

Ingredients	4 Portions	24 Portions
Sea bass, whole	1½ lb.	9 lb.
Chinese sweet pork sausages	2	12
Fresh scallops	¼ lb.	1½ lb.
Scallions, cut into ringlets	3	18
Water chestnuts	5 fresh (½ cup canned)	30 fresh (3 cups canned)
Soy oil	¼ cup + 2 Tbsp.	1¾ cups
Salt	As needed	As needed

Begin with a whole sea bass with head left on. "Butterfly" the bass by splitting it down the back to remove the backbone. Do not open the fish through the bottom, or "tummy," or it will fall apart when cooked. Thoroughly clean out the gills and any residual bones. Pat dry.

Prepare stuffing. With the metal blade of a food processor or in a meat grinder with coarse blade grind the sausages, scallops and water chestnuts separately, until each is the size of small niblets. Do not overprocess.

Combine the chopped sausages, scallops, chestnuts and scallions. Gently stuff the bass through the back.

Add oil to a wok or large heavy-bottomed frying pan, sprinkle with salt; gently rub fish with 2 Tbsp. of oil. Heat oil over medium flame; when hot, gently ease fish into pan, shaking pan or rocking wok from time to time to be sure the fish cooks evenly and to keep from sticking.

Cook for about 10 minutes on each side, turning fish gently using 2 large spatulas. Fish skin should be golden brown and unbroken.

To serve, transfer to a large platter and garnish with parsley or coriander.

FRIED RICE

The mixture can be pressed into cups and then unmolded for serving.

Ingredients	6 Portions	24 Portions
Eggs, beaten	2	8
Soy oil (for frying)	3 Tbsp.	¾ cup
Ham, pork, beef or shrimp, cooked, cooled, finely diced	1 cup	4 cups
Green onions, thinly sliced	6	24
Rice, cooked and thoroughly cooled	4 cups	16 cups
Soy sauce	2 Tbsp.	½ cup
Sugar	½ tsp.	2 tsp.
Salt	To taste	To taste

Fry eggs until firm; remove from heat and cut into shreds.

Return eggs to frying pan with meat and onion. Cook, stirring constantly for 3 to 4 minutes.

Add rice, soy sauce, sugar and salt. Serve hot.

STIR-FRIED MUSHROOMS

Can be served hot or at room temperature.

Ingredients	6 Portions	24 Portions
Button mushrooms	1 lb. small	4 lb.
Garlic, minced	3 cloves	12 cloves
Fresh ginger, cut into toothpick-size slivers	3–4 slices	12 slices
Soy sauce	2 Tbsp.	½ cup
Sherry	2 Tbsp.	½ cup
Szechwan sesame oil with hot chilies	Several drops	Several drops

| Chicken broth | 2 Tbsp. | ½ cup |
| Soybean oil | 2 Tbsp. | ½ cup |

Wipe mushrooms with a damp towel. If large, cut in half, but if small, leave whole.

Combine garlic, ginger, soy sauce, sherry, sesame oil and broth and set aside.

In a wok, heat the peanut oil, add mushrooms and stir-fry just until lightly browned.

Transfer mushrooms to a small, covered baking dish, add sauce and simmer gently for about 10 minutes.

These may be served warm, at room temperature or may be reheated.

Avocado and Shrimp
Groundnut Beef
Brown Rice with Mushrooms
Cherry Tomatoes
Jalebi Cookies

•

Fill avocado halves with shrimp which have marinated in a
vinaigrette dressing flavored with curry, and serve as an
appetizer/salad.

Cherry tomatoes warmed by lightly sautéing with butter and
thyme add a touch of color to the plate.

The dessert is an unusual sweet from northern India. Indian
chefs use a coconut shell with one hole in it, instead of a
funnel, to form the fancy spirals. The Pennsylvania Dutch make
a similar cookie called funnel cake.

GROUNDNUT BEEF

Based on the spicy braised meat patties known as frikkadels popular in South Africa.

Ingredients	4 Portions	24 Portions
Ground beef chuck	1 lb.	6 lb.
Cocktail peanuts, chopped	½ cup	3 cups
Bread crumbs, fresh	½ cup	3 cups
Onion, chopped	⅓ cup	2 cups
Coriander, ground	½ tsp.	1 Tbsp.
Salt	½ tsp.	1 Tbsp.
Nutmeg, ground	⅛ tsp.	¾ tsp.
Pepper	⅛ tsp.	¾ tsp.
Milk	¼ cup	1½ cups
Egg	1	6
Soy oil	1 Tbsp.	⅓ cup
Water	1 cup	6 cups
Beef bouillon	1 cube	6 cubes
Flour	1 Tbsp.	⅓ cup

In a large bowl, combine ground beef, peanuts, bread crumbs, onion, coriander, salt, nutmeg, pepper, milk and egg; mix well. Shape into oval patties, about 1-inch thick.

Heat oil in a large skillet. Add patties and brown well on both sides. Stir in ¾ (4½) cup water and bouillon cube(s). Bring to a boil. Reduce heat, cover and simmer 20 minutes. Blend together flour and remaining water. Add to skillet and cook, stirring, until thickened and boiling.

BROWN RICE WITH MUSHROOMS

A nice accompaniment for any kind of meal.

Ingredients	6 Portions	24 Portions
Mushrooms, fresh, sliced	2 cups	8 cups
Green onions, chopped finely with tops	½ cup	2 cups
Soy oil	2 Tbsp.	½ cup
Brown rice, cooked in beef broth	3 cups (1 cup raw)	12 cups (4 cups raw)
Salt	1 tsp.	4 tsp.

Sauté mushrooms and onions in oil until tender. Add rice and salt. Heat thoroughly. Fluff lightly with a fork.

JALEBI COOKIES

Saffron-colored flour spirals are deep-fried, then soaked in rose water syrup.

Ingredients	20 Cookies	60 Cookies
All-purpose flour	1½ cups	4½ cups
Saffron, crushed	Pinch	Pinch
Yogurt	2 Tbsp.	6 Tbsp.
Water, warm	1 cup	3 cups
Sugar	2 cups	6 cups
Water	2 cups	6 cups
Rose water	1 Tbsp.	3 Tbsp.
Oil for deep frying		

Sift flour into a mixing bowl. Add saffron and yogurt. Gradually pour in 1 (3) cup warm water. Keep mixing until a smooth batter is obtained. Cover and set aside in a warm place overnight.

Dissolve sugar in 2 (6) cups water. Boil 5 minutes. Simmer over medium-low heat 5 minutes. Add rose water and set aside.

Heat oil to 375°F for deep frying. Beat batter well, making sure it is free from lumps. Fill a funnel with a small opening (a little smaller than the thickness of a pencil) or a plastic catsup bottle with a nozzle.

With a rapid motion, squeeze the batter in a spiral into the hot oil. Fry 4 to 5 at one time until golden.

Soak the jalebis in the syrup 4 to 5 minutes. Remove from syrup and serve immediately.

Cauliflower/Cheese Soup
Swedish Salmon Loaf
Beet Salad with Cream Dressing
Cucumber Spears
Limpa Bread
Snip Cookies

•

Cauliflower/Cheese Soup can be made using either frozen or fresh, cooked cauliflower. If your cheese supplier carries Danish samsoe cheese, try it in this dish. (Samsoe or samsö is hard, white, sharp, slightly powdery and sweetish.)

Beet Salad has other vegetables, plus apples, in the wholesome mix—but the beets are the most noticeable because they turn everything red.

Limpa Bread is a somewhat sweet rye bread from the Scandinavian countries. The Norwegian Snip Cookies puff up as if two cookies had been placed together. Be careful, they're so rich and the temperature is so high that they burn easily.

CAULIFLOWER/CHEESE SOUP

A hearty soup that is quick and relatively easy to make.

Ingredients	6 Portions	24 Portions
Green onions, chopped (use only 1 inch of green stems)	1 bunch	4 bunches
Butter	2 Tbsp.	½ cup
Flour	2 Tbsp.	½ cup
Chicken broth	2 cups	2 quarts
Frozen cauliflower, thawed, sliced	1 pkg. (10 oz.)	4 pkg. (2½lb.)
Milk	2 cups	2 quarts
Cheddar or samsoe cheese, grated	2 cups	8 cups
Pale dry sherry, optional	2 Tbsp.	½ cup
Chives, chopped	1 Tbsp.	¼ cup

Sauté onion in butter until glazed. Add flour; cook 2 minutes. Slowly stir in broth.

Cook, stirring constantly, until thickened. Add cauliflower. Simmer 2 minutes. Stir in milk and cheese.

Heat until cheese melts. Stir in sherry, if desired.

Ladle into soup bowls. Garnish with chives.

SWEDISH SALMON LOAF

Can be baked in individual loaf pans or as a larger loaf, then sliced to serve.

Ingredients	6 Portions	24 Portions
Salmon, drained, flaked	1 can (1 lb.)	4 lb.
Salt	1 tsp.	1 Tbsp. + 1 tsp.
Eggs, beaten	2	8
Celery, finely chopped	1 cup	4 cups
Onion, finely chopped	½ cup	2 cups
Cracker crumbs	2 cups (about 44 medium)	8 cups
Milk	2 cups	2 quarts
Flour	¼ cup	1 cup

Preheat oven to 350°F.

Mix together salmon, salt, eggs, celery, onion and cracker crumbs.

Blend together milk and flour; cook and stir over medium heat until thick and bubbly. Continue cooking 1 minute. Add salmon mixture to milk.

Turn into a well-greased 8x4x3-inch loaf dish. Bake about 1 hour or until set in the center.

BEET SALAD with CREAM DRESSING

Potatoes, apples, carrots and beets together in a pretty mold.

Ingredients	6 Portions	24 Portions
Potatoes, cooked, peeled, diced	2 medium	8 medium
Tart apples, peeled, diced	2	8
Carrots, pared, cooked, diced	2	8
Onion, minced	¼ cup	1 cup
Dill pickles, finely minced	2 medium	8 medium
Beets, diced, drained	1 can (1 lb.)	4 lb.
Dairy sour cream	½ cup	2 cups
Salt	¼ tsp.	1 tsp.
White pepper	⅛ tsp.	½ tsp.
Lemon juice	2 Tbsp.	½ cup

In a large bowl, combine potatoes, apples, carrots, onion, pickles and beets.

Blend together sour cream, salt, pepper and lemon juice. Fold into vegetable mixture.

Pack into a lightly oiled, large bowl or into a ring mold. Chill several hours before serving.

Invert onto serving platter. If ring mold was used, place bowl of dressing (recipe follows) into center of ring. Garnish around edge with greens.

CREAM DRESSING

Ingredients	6 Portions	24 Portions
Whipping cream	1 cup	4 cups
Salt	Dash	⅛ tsp.
Sugar	1 Tbsp.	¼ cup
Lemon juice	2 Tbsp.	½ cup

Combine whipping cream, salt and sugar. Whip until soft peaks form. Stir in lemon juice until blended. Turn into small serving bowl.

May be garnished with chopped hardcooked eggs, green pepper strips, and sliced beets.

LIMPA BREAD

Sprinkle caraway seeds on the crust or serve the bread with butter flavored with caraway seeds or Kummel.

Ingredients	2 Loaves
Active dry yeast	2 pkg.
Warm water	½ cup
Sugar	½ cup
Light molasses	¼ cup
Soy oil	2 Tbsp.
Salt	2 tsp.
Orange peel, grated	2 tsp.
Hot water	1 cup
Medium rye flour, stirred	2½ cups
All-purpose flour, sifted	3½ to 4 cups

Preheat oven to 375°F.

Soften yeast in warm water.

In large bowl, combine sugar, molasses, oil, salt and orange peel. Add hot water and stir until sugar dissolves. Cool to lukewarm.

Stir in rye flour; beat well. Add softened yeast; mix well. Stir in all-purpose flour to make a soft dough. Continue kneading until smooth and satiny, about 10 minutes.

Place dough in lightly greased bowl, turning once to grease surface. Cover; let rise in warm place until double, about 45 minutes.

Punch down. Turn out on lightly floured surface; divide in 2 portions. Let rest 10 minutes.

Shape into 2 round loaves; place on greased baking sheets. Cover; let rise in warm place until double, about 30 minutes.

Bake 30 to 35 minutes. Place foil over tops last 10 minutes. For soft crust, brush with melted butter or margarine. Cool on rack.

SNIP COOKIES

Rich, diamond-shaped Norwegian cookies that melt in your mouth but are not sweet. If they don't puff during baking, they're rolled too thin.

Ingredients	2 Dozen cookies	4 Dozen cookies
Butter	1 cup	2 cups
Dairy sour cream	1 cup	2 cups
All-purpose flour, sifted	2 cups	4 cups
Vanilla or lemon extract	¼ tsp.	½ tsp.
Granulated sugar	¼ cup	½ cup

Preheat oven to 500°F.

Cut butter into flour as you would for pie crust; add sour cream, stirring with a fork. Roll (but not too thin) on a lightly floured board and cut into diamond shapes.

Place on a baking sheet and sprinkle with sugar. Bake about 5 minutes, or until very lightly browned.

NOTE: This is an old Norwegian recipe. If the cream is not rich enough, you may want to add a little extra butter.

Crudités
Tourtière (Pork Pie)
Pernod Peas in Sour Cream
Coffee Ice Cream with
Bittersweet Mocha Sauce

•

Nibble upon such crudités as cauliflowerets, zucchini rounds, the broccoli ends cut match-stick thin, and radishes made to fan out in cold water.

Tourtière is a French Canadian dish; the meat pie can be served hot as an entree, or cold slices can be served as an appetizer. Mushroom sauce is a suitable accompaniment when the dish is used as an entree.

Any licorice-flavored liqueur such as Pernod or Ouzo does wonderful things to green vegetables.

Buy or make coffee ice cream and serve with the Bittersweet Mocha Sauce.

TOURTIÈRE

A tasty pork pie that can be varied by the addition of minced garlic, celery salt or cooked mashed potatoes.

Ingredients	6 Pies	24 Pies
Onions, chopped	1 medium	4 medium
Salt	To taste	To taste
Sage	¾ tsp.	1 Tbsp.
Pork, ground, raw, lean	2¼ lb.	9 lb.
Water	¼ cup + 2 Tbsp.	1½ cups

Preheat oven to 450°F.

Combine ingredients in skillet and cook for 25 minutes. Cool.

Pour into a pie plate lined with unbaked piecrust and bake for 15 minutes, then reduce the oven to 350°F for 5 to 10 minutes, until nicely browned.

PERNOD PEAS IN SOUR CREAM

A cool way to serve peas.

Ingredients	8 Portions	24 Portions
Shelled peas, fresh or frozen	¾ lb. (about 2 cups)	2¼ lb. (about 6 cups)
Sour cream	½ cup	1½ cups
Horseradish	½ tsp.	1½ tsp.
Salt	¼ tsp.	¾ tsp.
Dry mint	⅛ tsp.	¼ tsp.
or	or	or
Fresh mint, chopped	½ tsp.	2 tsp.
Pernod	¼ tsp.	¾ tsp.
Scallions, thinly sliced, including green tops	2	6
Red apple, unpeeled, cored and finely chopped	½	1½

If fresh peas are used, cook them until barely tender and then cool. If frozen peas are used, turn them onto paper towels to thaw.

Combine remaining ingredients with peas. Chill.

BITTERSWEET MOCHA SAUCE

Ingredients	6 Portions	24 Portions
Semi-sweet chocolate	1 pkg. (6 oz.)	4 pkg. (24 oz.)
Unsweetened chocolate, melted	1 square (1 oz.)	4 squares (4 oz.)
Coffee-flavored liqueur	2 to 3 Tbsp.	⅔ cup
Heavy cream	½ cup	2 cups

Combine chocolate and liqueur in top of double boiler. When chocolate has melted, gradually stir in cream. For a thinner sauce use additional cream.

Serve hot over coffee ice cream.

Mixed Salad
Cornish Hens Valencienne
Beets in Sour Cream
Fruit and Coconut Balls

•

This casserole is planned for each person to have half a large Rock Cornish hen, plus Chorizo (Spanish sausages) and Canadian bacon. The rice cooks in wine and stock while the hens bake on top.

Beets in Sour Cream get their zest from the horseradish and onion; the dish can be heated and held in a double boiler while you're greeting your guests.

Fruit and Coconut Balls are a good idea at any time of year. Scoop any kind of ice cream or sherbet into balls, then roll in toasted coconut; cover and store in the freezer. They can be served with fruit in a sherbet dish or in a meringue shell.

CORNISH HENS VALENCIENNE

An elegant casserole.

Ingredients	4 Portions	24 Portions
Rock Cornish hens	2 large (1 lb. each)	12 large (1 lb. each)
Salt	To taste	To taste
Pepper	To taste	To taste
Butter	2 Tbsp.	¾ cup
Canadian bacon, cut in cubes	½ lb.	3 lb.
Chorizo sausages, cut in ¼-inch slices	6 oz.	2 lb.
White wine	1 cup	6 cups
Chicken or veal stock, or water	2¼ cups	3¾ quarts
Long grain and wild rice, mixed	6 oz.	2 lb.

Preheat oven to 350°F.

Cut hens in half, sprinkle with salt and pepper. Heat the butter and brown the birds on all sides; remove from pan. Brown bacon and sausage about 10 minutes, stirring constantly. Remove and drain well on paper toweling. Drain off all fat from the pan.

Add the wine and boil until reduced to ¼ cup (1½ cups). Add the stock or water and bring back to a boil. Stir in the bacon, sausage, rice, salt and pepper. Transfer to casserole and add the hens. Cover casserole and bake for 35 to 45 minutes or until the birds are tender; all the liquid should be absorbed by the rice.

Pile the rice on a platter, arrange the birds overlapping on top. Serve hot.

BEETS IN SOUR CREAM

Don't cook at too high a temperature, or the cream will curdle; just heat and hold in a double boiler.

Ingredients	4 Portions	24 Portions
Beets, sliced	3 cups	4½ quarts
Sour cream	½ cup	3 cups
Horseradish	1 Tbsp.	⅓ cup
Chives	1 Tbsp.	⅓ cup
Onion, grated	1 tsp.	2 Tbsp.
Salt	To taste	To taste

Combine ingredients and heat in a double boiler until warmed through.

Fresh Asparagus and Ham Soup
Tuna Brioche Ring
Crisp Crudités
Old-Fashioned Strawberry Shortcake

•

The asparagus tips and ham are cooked in the broth only seven minutes in this quick and easy soup.

Tuna Brioche isn't quick to make, but it doesn't require any kneading and there is only one rising period. When the brioche dough has risen, it is rolled into a rectangle and filled with a tuna and cheese mixture. Once baked, it can be served at room temperature or warm with Swiss Cheese Sauce. The brioche ring is large; it will make 12 servings.

Old-Fashioned Strawberry Shortcake with real, honest-to-goodness whipped cream can't be beat for a spring dessert. Add a little grated orange peel, orange-flavored liqueur or almond flavoring to the cream, and you'll beat the unbeatable.

FRESH ASPARAGUS AND HAM SOUP

The stalks flavor the smooth soup with the tender tips added last.

Ingredients	6 Portions	24 Portions
Fresh asparagus	1 lb.	4 lb.
Butter or margarine	1 Tbsp.	¼ cup
Small onion, finely chopped	1	4
Celery, finely chopped	1 stalk	4 stalk
Chicken broth	4 cups	1 gallon
Cooked ham, diced	1 cup	4 cups
Milk	½ cup	2 cups

Wash asparagus; break off stalk ends as far down as stalk snaps easily; discard ends. Cut off tips and reserve. Cut remainder of stalks into ½-inch pieces.

Melt butter in saucepan, add onion and celery; cook 2 minutes or until almost tender. Add cut-up asparagus stalks and chicken broth. Simmer, covered, 15 to 20 minutes, or until asparagus is very tender.

Ladle mixture into blender or food processor a little at a time and blend until very smooth.

Pour back into saucepan; add diced ham, milk and reserved asparagus tips. Simmer gently about 7 minutes, until asparagus tips are tender.

TUNA BRIOCHE RING

A rich, tender pastry conceals a tuna and cheese center.

Ingredients	12 Portions	24 Portions
NO-KNEAD PASTRY		
Milk	⅓ cup	⅔ cup
Butter or margarine	2 Tbsp.	¼ cup
Sugar	2 Tbsp.	¼ cup
Salt	1 tsp.	2 tsp.
Active dry yeast	1½ tsp. (½ pkg.)	1 pkg.
Warm water (110–120°F)	2 Tbsp.	¼ cup
Egg, slightly beaten	1	2
All-purpose flour, sifted	2 to 2¼ cups	4 to 4½ cups
TUNA FILLING		
Tuna in oil	2 cans (6½ or 7 oz. ea.)	4 cans (6½ or 7 oz. ea.)

Hard-cooked eggs	4	8
Swiss cheese, shredded	1 cup	2 cups
Stuffed green olives, chopped	½ cup	1 cup
Onion, minced	¼ cup	½ cup
Mayonnaise	¼ cup + 1 Tbsp., divided	½ cup + 2 Tbsp., divided
Worcestershire sauce	2 tsp.	1 Tbsp. + 1 tsp.
Pepper	⅛ tsp.	¼ tsp.
Parsley, chopped	½ cup	1 cup
Egg, lightly beaten	1	2
Milk	1 Tbsp.	2 Tbsp.
Sesame seeds	2 Tbsp.	¼ cup

In a small saucepan, heat milk, butter, sugar, and salt until butter melts. Cool to lukewarm.

In a large bowl, dissolve yeast in warm water. Add cooled milk mixture and egg. Beat in flour to make a soft dough. Place dough on lightly floured surface; shape into a smooth ball.

Place dough in greased bowl; turn greased side up. Cover; let rise in warm place until double in bulk, about 1½ hours.

Drain excess liquid from tuna; place tuna in a large bowl; break into flakes. Separate egg whites from yolks; reserve yolks. Chop egg whites; add to tuna. Add cheese, olives, onion, ¼ cup (½ cup))mayonnaise, Worcestershire sauce and pepper. Mix thoroughly.

In a small bowl, mash reserved egg yolks; stir in parsley and remaining mayonnaise.

Preheat oven to 350°F.

On floured surface, roll dough into a rectangle 7 x 22 inches. Spread tuna mixture on the dough, leaving a 1-inch border along one long side.

Spoon egg yolk mixture in a thin strip over the tuna mixture, along the side *opposite* the border.

Next, roll dough, jelly roll fashion, beginning with the side spread with the egg yolk mixture.

Shape into a circle, seam-side down, and pinch ends together. Place in a greased 9-inch springform pan, pressing gently against sides of pan.

Beat egg and milk together; brush over pastry. Bake 15 minutes.

Brush again with egg mixture; sprinkle with sesame seeds. Bake 20 to 30 minutes longer until evenly browned.

If desired, garnish with a "bow" fashioned with cut-out pieces of pimiento. Serve at room temperature or warm with *Swiss Cheese Sauce* (recipe follows).

SWISS CHEESE SAUCE

Swiss, rather than cheddar, sauces the Tuna Brioche Ring.

Ingredients	2¾ Cups	5¼ Cups
Butter or margarine	¼ cup	½ cup
Onion, minced	⅓ cup	⅔ cup
Flour	¼ cup	½ cup
Milk	2½ cups	5 cups
Worcestershire sauce	¾ tsp.	1½ tsp.
Salt	¼ tsp.	½ tsp.
Tabasco pepper sauce	⅛ tsp.	¼ tsp.
Swiss cheese, shredded	¾ cup	1½ cups
Parsley, chopped	2 Tbsp.	¼ cup

In medium saucepan, melt butter; sauté onions in butter until tender. Blend in flour; cook over low heat 2 minutes, stirring constantly. Remove from heat; gradually stir in milk, Worcestershire sauce, salt and Tabasco.

Cook over medium heat, stirring constantly, until sauce thickens and comes to a boil. Add cheese; stir until melted. Do not allow to boil. Remove from heat; stir in chopped parsley.

OLD-FASHIONED STRAWBERRY SHORTCAKE

A large biscuit round, split, then layered with berries and whipped cream.

BERRIES AND CREAM

Ingredients	8 Portions	24 Portions
Strawberries, washed and hulled	two 1-pint baskets	six 1-pint baskets
Sugar	½ cup + 2 tsp.	1½ cups + 2 Tbsp.
Heavy cream	1 cup	3 cups
Orange rind, grated	½ tsp.	1½ tsp.

Reserve a whole berry for each shortcake. Slice strawberries into a bowl; sprinkle with ½ cup (1½ cups) sugar and let stand at room temperature. If desired, crush berries slightly.

Whip cream with 2 tsp. (2 Tbsp.) sugar; refrigerate.

SHORTCAKE

Ingredients	1 Cake	3 Cakes
Unsifted all-purpose flour	2 cups	6 cups
Sugar	⅓ cup	1 cup
Baking powder	1 Tbsp. + 1 tsp.	¼ cup
Salt	½ tsp.	1½ tsp.
Nutmeg	½ tsp.	1½ tsp.
Soft butter or margarine	½ cup	1½ cups
Egg	1	3
Milk	⅓ cup	1 cup

Preheat oven to 450°F.

Mix flour, sugar, baking powder, salt and nutmeg in large bowl. Cut in butter until mixture resembles coarse meal.

Beat together egg and milk, add to flour mixture and stir just until blended. Pat into a 9-inch round(s) on a greased baking sheet and bake 15 minutes or until golden brown.

Let cool about 2 minutes, then split shortcake with a serrated knife into two layers. Spread a little softened butter on the bottom cut side and the top of the top layer. Place bottom layer on a serving plate. Spread with two-thirds of whipped cream and top with two-thirds of strawberries and syrup. Add top layer of shortcake, spread with almost all of remaining whipped cream and top with remaining berries and syrup. Garnish top with a dollop of whipped cream and reserved whole berries.

FIVE
Ethnic Fare from Everywhere

With Americans mixing and matching ethnic strains in ever-increasing numbers, and traveling the globe with ease, there has been an increasing awareness of ethnic foods. We've come to love Baklava, Kibbi and Feta Cheese with the fervor once reserved only for Tacos, Tamales and Egg Rolls.

Not only have we weaned our youngsters away from a strictly meat-and-potatoes diet, but we've managed to convince grandpa and grandma, too. The more variety we have in our meals, the more interesting, and inexpensive, they become.

Every nation has a variation on the meat pie theme; most have some sort of a crepe, and there are more ethnic dishes based on chicken than any broiler man ever dreamed possible.

When your purse won't finance a trip to another land, travel with it to the grocery store and buy an inexpensive substitute–the ingredients for an ethnic luncheon. At least you'll know you can trust the water, and the kitchen will meet your standard for cleanliness.

Baba Ghanouj
Shish Kebab
Lavash
Baklava

•

Everyone loves Shish Kebab and you can do the broiling outdoors, in your fireplace, or in the range. When you have a crowd for lunch, let them cook their own skewers.

Lavash is a crisp, wafer-like bread that you bake in huge sheets. It's spectacular to serve if you do not break the sheets, but arrange them on a platter or in a large basket and let guests help themselves. The Baba Ghanouj can be scooped up with the Lavash—or with store-bought pita bread.

Baklava can be purchased, but since the arrival of phyllo dough in the freezer section of grocery stores, it is easy to make.

BABA GHANOUJ

Eggplant with sesame oil—serve as an appetizer or a salad.

Ingredients	4 Portions	24 Portions
Eggplant, dark-skinned	1 medium	6
Garlic	2 cloves	12 cloves
Salt	To taste	To taste
Sesame oil	3 Tbsp.	1 cup
Juice from lemons	2	12
Water	2 Tbsp.	¾ cup
Pine nuts	2 Tbsp.	¾ cup
Pomegranate seeds, optional	2 Tbsp.	¾ cup
Parsley, chopped	2 Tbsp.	¾ cup

Broil whole eggplant with skin on, turning it frequently. Remove skin under cold water and mash eggplant.

Pound the garlic with salt; add sesame oil, lemon juice and water. Then mix with eggplant and salt.

Spread on a platter and garnish with pine nuts, pomegranate seeds and parsley.

SHISH KEBAB

Lamb or beef marinated and broiled on skewers.

Ingredients	4 Portions	24 Portions
Leg of lamb, boned and lean or		
Round steak	1 lb.	6 lb.
Onion, quartered	½	3
Red wine	½ cup	3 cups
Oil	1½ tsp.	3 Tbsp.
Dried mint	1 tsp.	2 Tbsp.
Salt and pepper	To taste	To taste
Green peppers, sliced in squares	2	12
Cherry tomatoes	8	48

Cut lamb or steak into 1½ inch squares.

Make a marinade of onions, wine, oil and mint in a deep dish and marinate meat for at least 2 hours, preferably overnight.

Season when ready to broil. Arrange lamb squares on skewers, alternating with onions, pepper slices, and tomato.

Broil slowly over hot charcoal or in broiler about 10 minutes.

LAVASH

Although it looks like matzo it differs greatly, having both salt and leavening.

Ingredients

Flour, all-purpose	**3 lb.**
Yeast cake or package	**1**
Salt	**2 tsp.**
Water, lukewarm to make a stiff dough	

Dissolve yeast in 2 cups of warm water.

Sift flour and salt into a large bowl. Make a depression in the center of the flour and gradually work in dissolved yeast and enough additional water to make a stiff dough.

Knead well, place in bowl, cover, and let stand for about 3 hours. Punch dough down and let rise again.

Sift flour over a large board or table top, and spread evenly over surface. Now pinch off pieces of dough about the size of a large egg. With a rolling pin roll dough out into a large sheet, as large as your oven will accommodate. Dough should be about ⅛-inch thick.

Place on a cookie sheet, or the bottom of the oven, and bake at 400°F for about 3 minutes. Then place under broiler to brown the top lightly, watching all the time to keep from burning.

Repeat this process until all the dough has been used up. Store in a dry place.

BAKLAVA

The favorite dessert of the Middle East—it freezes very well.

Ingredients	*20 Pieces*
Ground walnuts	**3 cups**
Confectioners' sugar	**¼ cup**
Cinnamon	**¼ tsp.**
Phyllo pastry	**1 lb.**
Butter, melted	**1 cup**

Mix together walnuts, confectioners' sugar and cinnamon.

Unwrap phyllo. If edges are dry, cut them away. To keep phyllo moist, cover unused part with a damp towel.

Brush bottom and sides of 13x9x2-inch baking pan with some of the butter. Arrange 1 sheet of phyllo in the bottom of pan, overlapping all sides so phyllo fits pan. Brush lightly with butter. Trim the remaining phyllo sheets to 13 inches long. The sides will be folded in to fit the pan.

211

Place one phyllo sheet in pan; brush lightly with melted butter. Fold in sides; brush sides with butter. Continue adding a sheet of phyllo and brushing with butter 5 more times.

Spread ¾ cup of nut mixture on top of pastry. Add 4 more sheets of pastry in the above manner. Spread with ¾ cup nut mixture. Continue layering, brushing and spreading with nut filling 2 more times, each time using 4 sheets of phyllo and ¾ cup nut mixture.

Add 5 sheets of phyllo in the above manner but folding the sides of the last sheet under to give a finished appearance. Brush top with butter.

Cutting halfway to bottom of pan, make three lengthwise cuts dividing the pan into 4 rows. Make diagonal cuts about 2 inches apart to make diamond shaped pieces of pastry.

Bake in 350°F (moderate) oven 1¼ hours. If the top begins to get too brown, cover with a piece of foil placed loosely over Baklava.

While Baklava bakes prepare syrup following recipe below. Remove baked Baklava from oven and while it is still hot, slowly pour syrup over pastry. Let stand at least 24 hours before serving. Baklava does not require refrigeration. Makes 20 pieces (about 4 pounds).

For smaller pieces make 5 lengthwise cuts halfway to bottom of pan. Slash each row diagonally on the surface making cuts about 1 inch apart to form diamond pattern. Makes 64 pieces.

BAKLAVA SYRUP

Ingredients

Sugar	1½ cups
Water	1 cup
Corn syrup, light	1 cup
Lemon juice	2 Tbsp.
Cinnamon stick	1
Rosewater, to taste, optional	

Mix together all ingredients in 3-quart saucepan. Bring to boil, stirring constantly, and boil 15 minutes. Remove cinnamon stick. Makes about 2 cups.

If rosewater is used, omit lemon juice and cinnamon stick.

Salted Macadamia Nuts
Luau Platter
Hawaiian Fruit Bread
Coconut Ice Cream or Lime Sherbet

•

Chicken and ribs baked and served hot or cold with fruits colorfully arranged on bamboo skewers, broiled and rolled in coconut, make a pretty platter or plate. The fruit bread can be served both with the entree and with the dessert.

When you do the meat and the baking ahead, and have the fruits threaded on the skewers and ready to pop into the oven, there is very little to do at the last minute.

LUAU PLATTER

Chicken, ribs and fruit, glazed and broiled, then rolled in coconut.

Ingredients	6 Portions	24 Portions
CHICKEN AND RIBS		
Bottled spicy, sweet French dressing	1 cup	4 cups
Honey	1 Tbsp.	¼ cup
Peach preserves	½ cup	2 cups
Soy sauce	1 tsp.	1 Tbsp. + 1 tsp.
Spareribs (cut into individual ribs)	12 (2 lb.)	48 (8 lb.)
Chicken legs	6 (1½ lb.)	24 (6 lb.)
SKEWERED FRUITS WITH COCONUT		
Bananas, in chunks	3	12
Maraschino cherries, optional	6	24
Pineapple chunks, fresh or canned	12	48
Peach halves	1	4
Pear quarters	12	48
Apple wedges	12	48
Coconut, shredded		

Preheat oven to 375°F.

In small bowl, combine French dressing, honey, preserves and soy sauce. In foil-lined jelly roll pan, bake spareribs 30 minutes; drain.

Add chicken and bake, basting both spareribs and chicken frequently with dressing glaze (reserve some for fruit) 45 minutes or until chicken is tender.

Alternately thread fruits on small bamboo skewers. Bake 10 minutes, basting frequently with reserved dressing glaze; roll in coconut.

Serve with spareribs and chicken.

HAWAIIAN FRUIT BREAD

Can be served spread with cream cheese sparked with rum or Cointreau.

Ingredients	2 Loaves	6 Loaves
Granulated sugar	2 cups	6 cups
Unsifted all-purpose flour, spooned lightly into cup and leveled	4 cups	12 cups

Baking powder	2 tsp.	2 Tbsp.
Salt	1 tsp.	1 Tbsp.
Chopped dates	1 cup	3 cups
Chopped dried apricots	1 cup	3 cups
Chopped walnuts	1 cup	3 cups
Eggs	2	6
Orange juice	1½ cups	4½ cups
Orange-flavored liqueur	¼ cup	¾ cup
Dark rum	½ cup	1½ cups
Baking soda	2 tsp.	2 Tbsp.
Butter or margarine, melted	2 Tbsp.	6 Tbsp.

Preheat oven to 350°F.

In a large mixing bowl, stir together the sugar, flour, baking powder and salt. Mix in dates, apricots and walnuts.

In another bowl, beat eggs and combine with remaining ingredients in the order listed. Add the wet ingredients to the dry and stir just until combined; do not overmix.

Pour into well-greased bread pans and bake 1 hour and 10 minutes or until a toothpick inserted in center of loaf comes out clean.

Limerick Soup
Corned Beef
Irish Soda Bread
Horseradish in Sour Cream
Almond Wine Biscuits
Tea

•

Few people can resist a hearty soup served with good home-baked soda bread and corned beef. The stock from cooking the corned beef is transformed into Limerick Soup when vegetables are added.

Corned beef gets added zest when served with a sauce made by flavoring sour cream with horseradish and mustard.

Almond Wine Biscuits are lovely with tea or with wine.

LIMERICK SOUP

A hearty soup for autumn lunches.

Ingredients	1 Quart	6 Quarts
Onions, yellow	⅓ lb.	2 lb.
Butter	2 tsp.	4 Tbsp.
Stock, from corned beef	2½ cups	1 gallon
Potatoes, sliced thin	1 lb.	6 lb.
Celery, minced	3 Tbsp.	1 cup
Carrots, diced	3 Tbsp.	1 cup
Green pepper, cut julienne	¼	1½
Green cabbage, shredded	⅙ lb.	1 lb.
Bouquet Garni		
Corned beef, minced	⅙ lb.	1 lb.
Milk, warmed	¾ cup	1 quart
Chives, chopped	1 Tbsp.	⅓ cup

Slice onions, and sauté lightly in butter until soft, but not golden. Add stock from corned beef, potatoes sliced thin, minced celery, diced carrots, green pepper and cabbage. Add salt and pepper to taste, and bouquet garni tied in cheesecloth.

Bring to boil. Add minced corned beef scraps and simmer until potatoes are done (about 40 minutes). Remove bouquet. Add warm milk and chopped chives. Mix well.

IRISH SODA BREAD

Firm enough to hold together for sandwiches.

Ingredients	1 Loaf	3 Loaves
All-purpose flour, unsifted	4 cups	12 cups
Baking soda	1 tsp.	1 Tbsp.
Salt	1 tsp.	1 Tsp.
Sugar	1 tsp.	1 Tbsp.
Buttermilk or sour milk	1½ cups	4½ cups

Preheat oven to 425°F.

Stir together flour, baking soda, salt and sugar. Add buttermilk and stir until barely combined.

Turn onto floured surface and knead lightly to shape round loaves.

Place on lightly oiled baking sheet. Cut a deep cross across tops, letting the cuts go over the sides of the bread.

Bake 45 minutes or until loaf sounds hollow when tapped on the bottom.

ALMOND WINE BISCUITS

Sherry, anise, lemon and almonds flavor these short cookies.

Ingredients	1 Dozen	4 Dozen
Flour, all-purpose sifted	1 cup	4 cups
Salt	⅛ tsp.	½ tsp.
Shortening, soft	½ cup	2 cups
Sugar, granulated	⅓ cup	1⅓ cup
Egg yolks	2	8
Anise extract	¼ tsp.	1 tsp.
Lemon rind, grated	½	2
Almonds, coarsely ground	½ cup	2 cups
Sherry	¼ cup	1 cup
Almonds, coarsely ground	⅓ cup	1⅓ cup

Preheat oven to 400°F.

Sift together flour and salt.

Mix, until creamy, shortening, sugar, and yolks. Add anise, rind, ½ (2) cups almonds. Mix in sherry alternately with flour mixture.

Drop by tablespoonfuls onto almonds; toss until well-coated with nuts.

Shape with spoon into 1½-inch rounds, ½-inch thick. Bake until golden, 1-inch apart on well-greased baking sheets.

Toasted, Salted Melon Seeds
or Salted Almonds
Plum Wine
Shrimp with Snow Peas
Watercress Salad
Lichi Nuts with Candied Ginger Zest

•

This can be a nice show-off luncheon if you have an electric wok. The Shrimp with Snow Peas takes only a few moments to make, and the Watercress Salad (based upon a Korean salad with a tongue-tingling dressing) is a light accompaniment.

Toasted, Salted Melon Seeds are available at most specialty shops and go well with the Plum Wine as an appetizer. If you don't fancy the sweet wine, any favorite beverage will serve.

Lichi Nuts can be purchased in a can, chilled and sprinkled with the very thinly sliced candied ginger.

SHRIMP WITH SNOW PEAS

This dish can be quickly prepared at the table if you have
an electric wok.

Ingredients	4 Portions	24 Portions
Large raw shrimp	16	96
Sugar	½ tsp.	1 Tbsp.
Soy sauce	1 tsp.	2 Tbsp.
Cornstarch	1½ tsp.	3 Tbsp.
Water	1 Tbsp.	⅓ cup
Soy oil	3 Tbsp.	1 cup + 2 Tbsp.
Salt	½ tsp.	1 Tbsp.
Chicken broth	⅓ cup	2 cups
Water chestnuts, thinly sliced	½ cup	3 cups
Snow peas, fresh or frozen	1½ cups	9 cups
Onion, cut in half crosswise, then cut in small wedges	½ cup	3 cups
Celery, cut crosswise in ¼-inch slices	1 cup	6 cups

Cut shrimp in half lengthwise and remove the vein.

Combine sugar, soy sauce, cornstarch and water, eliminating all
lumps.

Heat oil over high heat; add salt. Cover bottom with shrimp, stirring
and cooking 1 minute, or until shrimp turns pink and white. Remove
and do remaining shrimp.

Add remaining ingredients, sauce and return shrimp to pan. Cover
and cook 1½ minutes; remove cover to stir once or twice.

Serve at once with or without rice.

WATERCRESS SALAD

This Oriental salad-relish goes well with any dish from that part of
the world.

Ingredients	4 Portions	24 Portions
Watercress, washed, drained	2 bunches	12 bunches
Scallions, with tops, chopped	4	24
Pepper	¼ tsp.	1½ tsp.
Sugar	1½ tsp.	3 Tbsp.
Soy sauce	2 Tbsp.	¾ cup
Cider vinegar	1½ Tbsp.	½ cup
Dried red chili, 1-inch long	1	3
Sesame seed, crushed, toasted	1 tsp.	2 Tbsp.

Cut cress into 2-inch lengths. Mix with the chopped scallions, pepper, salt, sugar, soy sauce, vinegar and chili (which can be crushed if you prefer a *hot* dressing).

At serving time pour the dressing over the watercress and sprinkle with sesame seed.

NOTE: Place sesame seed in a heavy pan and cook over medium heat about 10 minutes, stirring until golden brown. Turn toasted seed into a mortar or an electric blender. Add 1 tsp. salt for each 1 cup of seed and crush. May be kept in a tightly covered jar.

Peppers Stuffed with Eggplant
White Truffle Fettucine
Fennel Sticks
Wine Poached Pears

•

Pepper shells filled with eggplant can be served hot or cold, but the White Truffle Fettucine with fresh basil, prosciutto and truffles can only be served piping hot.

Any kind of bread stick or Italian bread can replace the Fennel Sticks on the menu, but Fennel Sticks are really not difficult to make and the aroma of the fennel is worth any amount of trouble.

Wine Poached Pears can be done well ahead. Don't use your finest wine for poaching, something a bit sweet is particularly nice.

PEPPERS STUFFED WITH EGGPLANT

Serve hot or cold as an appetizer or with an entree.

Ingredients	4 Portions	24 Portions
Red or green bell peppers	2 large	12
Water, boiling	As needed	As needed
Eggplant, medium-size, regular	1	6
Olive oil	½ cup	3 cups
Garlic, minced or mashed	1 clove	6 cloves
Seasoned crumbs	¼ cup	1½ cups
Lemon wedges	As needed	As needed

Preheat oven to 375°F.

Cut peppers in half lengthwise and remove stems, seeds, and pith. Immerse in rapidly boiling water to cover and remove when water returns to boil; drain well. Arrange open side up in a rimmed baking pan, side by side. Trim stem from eggplant and discard.

Cut eggplant in ¾-inch cubes. Combine with 6 Tbsp. (2¼ cups) of the oil and the garlic in a large frying pan. Cook, stirring with a wide spatula, over medium heat until eggplant is lightly browned and moist looking, about 10 minutes.

Divide hot cooked eggplant evenly among the pepper half shells. Sprinkle eggplant evenly with the seasoned crumbs and drizzle with remaining olive oil.

Bake, uncovered for 30 minutes. Cool to room temperature; serve within 6 hours. Accompany with lemon wedges to squeeze over individual servings.

WHITE TRUFFLE FETTUCINE

A show-off dish for a host or a Captain.

Ingredients	4–5 Portions	20–25 Portions
Prosciutto	2 oz.	10 oz.
Basil, fresh and chopped	1 Tbsp.	¼ cup + 1 Tbsp.
Light cream or half-and-half	1 cup	1 quart + 1 cup
Italian tomato sauce	1 oz. (canned)	5 oz.
Garlic, crushed	1 small clove	5 small cloves
Black pepper	To taste	To taste
White truffles	1 can	5 cans
Parmesan cheese (preferably Parmesan and Romano in a 4:1 ratio)	½ cup	2½ cups

Butter	1 Tbsp.	5 Tbsp.
Fettucine or wide noodles	2 cups, cooked	10 cups, cooked

Shred prosciutto, remove all fat, sauté lightly. In the last couple of minutes, add the basil and sauté for 2 or 3 minutes longer; keep warm.

In a quart measuring cup, put light cream or half-and-half, tomato sauce, crushed garlic, and grind in black pepper liberally. Also add the water from the truffles and a few ounces of grated cheese to thicken somewhat.

Cook the fettucine in boiling water for about 8 minutes, tasting a strand to make sure it is *al dente,* not mushy or overcooked. Drain in a colander (do not pour water over it).

Pour the boiling water out of the kettle in which the fettucine was cooked. Place some butter in the bottom of the kettle and return the fettucine from the colander to the pot over a very low heat. Add the sauce from the quart cup, mixing constantly, and grind in more pepper and more grated cheese. At the last minute, add the thinly sliced truffles. Serve on hot plates.

NOTE: Because the cheese and fettucine are very salty, do *not* add salt.

FENNEL BREAD STICKS

The same seed that flavors mild Italian pork sausage makes these crisp bread sticks appealingly aromatic.

Ingredients	7 dozen
Dry yeast, active	1 package
Water, warm	¾ cup
Salad oil	¾ cup
Beer	¾ cup
Salt	1½ tsp.
Fennel seed	1 Tbsp.
All-purpose flour, unsifted	4½ cups
Egg, beaten with	1
Water	1 Tbsp.

Preheat oven to 325°F.

In a large bowl, soften yeast in the ¾ cup warm water. Add salad oil, beer, salt, and fennel seed. With a wooden spoon, beat in 3½ cups of the flour.

On a board or pastry cloth, spread remaining 1 cup flour; turn out soft dough. Knead using this technique: lift edge of the dough, coated well with flour, and fold toward center, avoiding contact with sticky part of

224

dough. Continue folding toward center and kneading, turning the dough as you work, until it is smooth and elastic. Place the dough in a bowl, cover, and let rise until double. Knead air from dough.

Pinch off 1½-inch-diameter lumps and roll each to 18-inch long ropes. Cut each rope in half. Set wire racks on baking sheets and place ropes across them, ½ inch apart.

Brush ropes with egg-water mixture. Bake for about 35 minutes or until evenly browned. Cool, then wrap airtight and store at room temperature.

WINE POACHED PEARS

Poached pears standing in their own sweet cooking liquid
are beautiful.

Ingredients	6 Portions	24 Portions
Firm-ripe medium to large pears, peeled	6	24
Dry red wine	1¾ cups	7 cups
Sugar	1 cup	4 cups
Anise seed	¼ tsp.	1 tsp.
Whole cinnamon sticks	2	8
Unpeeled, lemon slices	2 or 3, thin	10, thin

In a saucepan large enough to hold the pears side by side, combine the wine, sugar, anise, cinnamon, and lemon. Bring to a boil, stirring until sugar is dissolved.

Remove core from blossom ends of the pears, leaving stem in place. Set fruit into boiling syrup and boil, covered, about 8 to 10 minutes, turning fruit occasionally so all portions are at times in the syrup.

When fruit is heated through and still holds its shape, lift from syrup with a slotted spoon and transfer to a serving dish.

Boil syrup at high heat, uncovered, until reduced to ¾ to 1 cup (3 to 4 cups). Pour hot syrup over and around pears. Serve warm or at room temperature.

Potted Shrimp
Veal and Ham Pie
English Cucumber Salad
The Queen's Trifle
Earl Grey Tea

•

This menu is ideal for a hot summer day or a picnic lunch, providing you keep The Queen's Trifle cold. Perhaps a noontime picnic on the patio is the answer.

The Queen's Trifle is the recipe of a friend, award-winning chef Fritz Sonnenschmidt. Though Fritz was born in Bavaria, he cooked at one time for Britain's Queen Mother and this dessert was one of her favorites.

POTTED SHRIMP

Potted shrimp are delicious served with hot toast as an appetizer.

Ingredients	6 Portions	24 Portions
Butter, cut into ¼-inch bits	½ lb.	2 lb.
Mace	½ tsp.	2 tsp.
Cayenne pepper	⅛ tsp.	½ tsp.
Salt	1 tsp.	1 Tbsp + 1 tsp.
Tabasco	Dash	Dash
Fresh shrimp, tiny shelled, cooked	1 lb. or 2 cups	4 lb.

Clarify ¼ lb. (1 lb.) of the butter by melting it slowly over low heat. Skim off the surface foam and let the butter rest off the heat for a minute or two. Then spoon the clear butter on top into a heavy 6 to 8-inch skillet and discard the milky solids at the bottom of the saucepan.

Melt the remaining butter over moderate heat in a heavy saucepan. When the foam begins to subside, stir in the mace, cayenne pepper, salt, and Tabasco. Add the shrimp, turning them about with a spoon to coat them evenly.

Spoon the mixture into 4-ounce individual baking dishes or custard cups, dividing the shrimp equally among them. Seal by pouring a thick layer of the clarified butter over each.

Refrigerate the shrimp overnight or for at least 6 hours.

VEAL AND HAM PIE

Slices are particularly attractive with hard-cooked eggs running down the center and pickled walnuts flanking the eggs.

Ingredients	8 Portions (1 Pie)	24 Portions (3 Pies)
Butter, softened	2 Tbsp.	6 Tbsp.
Veal, lean & boneless, cut into ¼-inch cubes	2 lb.	6 lb.
Ham, lean & smoked, cut into ¼-inch cubes	1 lb.	3 lb.
Parsley, finely chopped	¼ cup	¾ cup
Brandy	6 Tbsp.	1 cup + 2 Tbsp.
Chicken or beef stock, fresh or canned	6 Tbsp.	1 cup + 2 Tbsp.
Lemon juice	2 Tbsp.	¼ cup + 2 Tbsp.
Lemon peel, grated fine	1 tsp.	1 Tbsp.

Sage leaves, dried and crumbled	1 tsp.	1 Tbsp.
Salt	2 tsp.	2 Tbsp.
Black pepper, freshly ground	¼ tsp.	¾ tsp.
Eggs, hard-cooked	4	12
Pickled walnuts (optional)	8–10	24–30
Egg yolk combined with heavy	1	3
cream	1 Tbsp.	3 Tbsp.
Gelatin, unflavored	1 envelope	3 envelopes
Chicken stock, fresh or canned	2 cups	6 cups

Preheat oven to 350°F.

Coat the bottom and sides of a 10x5x4-inch loaf mold with the butter. Set aside.

In a large bowl, combine the veal, ham, parsley, brandy, stock, lemon juice, peel, sage, salt and pepper. Toss the ingredients about with a spoon until thoroughly mixed.

Break off about one-third of the hot water pastry (recipe follows) and set it aside. On a lightly floured surface, roll out the remaining pastry into a rectangle about 20 inches long x 10 inches wide and ¼-inch thick. Gently press the pastry into the mold. Roll the pin over the rim to trim off the excess pastry.

Spoon enough of the veal and ham mixture into the pastry shell to fill it a little less than half full. Arrange the hard-cooked eggs in a single row down the center of the mold, and line up the pickled walnuts, if you are using them, on both sides of the eggs. Cover the eggs with the remaining meat mixture, filling the shell to within 1 inch of the top.

Roll the reserved pastry into a 4x13-inch rectangle, ¼ inch thick. Lift it over the top of the mold. Trim off excess with a small knife and, with the tines of a fork or your fingers crimp the pastry to secure it to the rim of the mold.

Cut a 1-inch round hole in the center of the pie(s).

Roll out the scraps of pastry and cut them into leaf and flower shapes. Moisten their bottom sides with the egg-and-cream mixture and arrange on the pie. Brush the entire surface with the egg-and-cream mixture.

Bake the pie in the middle of the oven for 2 hours, or until the top is a deep golden brown. Remove from the oven and cool for 15 minutes.

Sprinkle the gelatin over 2 (6) cups of cold chicken stock in saucepan and let it soften for 2 or 3 minutes. Then set the pan over low heat and cook, stirring constantly, until the gelatin dissolves completely. Pour the gelatin through a funnel into the opening of the pie(s).

Cool the pie to room temperature, then refrigerate for at least 6 hours, or until the aspic is set. Ideally the pie should be removed from the refrigerator about 30 minutes before being served.

To unmold and serve the pie, run the blade of a sharp knife around the inside edges of the mold and dip the bottom of the mold in hot water. Wipe the mold dry, place an inverted serving plate over it, and grasping mold and plate together firmly, quickly turn them over. Rap the plate on a table and the pie should slide out easily.

Turn the pie over and serve, cut into ½-inch thick slices.

HOT WATER PASTRY

Ingredients	1 Pie	3 Pies
Flour, all-purpose	2½ cups	7½ cups
Salt	¼ tsp.	¾ tsp.
Lard	5 Tbsp.	1 cup
Milk	3 Tbsp.	½ cup
Water	1 Tbsp.	3 Tbsp.

In a deep bowl, combine the flour and salt. Warm the lard, milk and water in a saucepan over moderate heat, and stir until the lard melts.

Beat the mixture, a few tablespoons at a time, into the flour, and continue to beat until the dough can be gathered into a compact ball.

On a lightly floured surface, knead the dough for 2 or 3 minutes by pressing it down, pushing it forward, and folding it back on itself until it is smooth and elastic. Again gather it into a ball.

Place it in a bowl and place a dampened kitchen towel over it. Let the dough rest for 30 minutes before using.

ENGLISH CUCUMBER SALAD

An excellent salad for meals which include ham, pork or fish.

Ingredients	6 Portions	24 Portions
Cucumbers	3	12
Mayonnaise	¾ cup	3 cups
Chives, chopped	1½ tsp.	2 Tbsp.
Vinegar, white	¼ cup	1 cup
Salt	½ tsp.	2 tsp.
Pepper	To taste	To taste
Onion, finely diced	½	2
Oil	¼ cup	1 cup

Peel the cucumbers and slice them thinly.

Combine the mayonnaise, chives, vinegar, salt, pepper, and onion and add them to the cucumbers. Mix the ingredients well.

Allow the mixture to rest for 30 minutes.

Adjust the seasoning to taste, then add the oil.

THE QUEEN'S TRIFLE

Ingredients	6 Portions	24 Portions
Pound Cake	½ lb.	2 lb.
Raspberry jam	¼ cup	1 cup
Almonds, sliced	½ cup	2 cups
Sugar	⅓ cup	1⅓ cup
Brandy	¼ cup	1 cup
Sherry, dry	¼ cup	1 cup
Cream, heavy	1 cup	1 quart
Sugar, superfine	1 Tbsp.	¼ cup
Raspberries, frozen or fresh	1 cup	4 cups
Custard sauce (see recipe below)	1½ cups	6 cups

Cut the pound cake into ½-inch slices and spread the jam over the slices.

Arrange the slices in a glass serving bowl. Sprinkle the almonds over each layer.

Dissolve the sugar in the brandy and sherry; heat until the sugar is completely dissolved. Cool the syrup and pour over the pound cake.

Whip the cream until stiff, and add the superfine sugar.

Scatter the raspberries over the cake, saving a dozen for decoration at the end. Spread the custard over the top.

Pipe the whipped cream all around the cake and decorate with the remaining raspberries.

CUSTARD SAUCE

Ingredients	1½ Cups	6 Cups
Vanilla bean	¼ stick	1 stick
Milk, boiled	¾ cup	3 cups
Sugar, granulated	½ cup	2 cups
Egg yolks	3	12
Gelatine, unflavored	1 Tbsp.	¼ cup
Cream, heavy	¼ cup	1 cup
Sugar, confectioners'	2 Tbsp.	½ cup
Vanilla sugar	1 tsp.	1 Tbsp. + 1 tsp.
or	or	or
Sugar	1 tsp.	1 Tbsp. + 1 tsp.
Vanilla extract	1–2 drops	4–5 drops

Place the vanilla bean in the boiled milk to steep.

Mix the granulated sugar and egg yolks in a saucepan. Dilute the gelatine with some of the milk in which the vanilla bean has been steeped. Dilute the sugar and egg yolks with the rest of the milk. Combine the gelatine and the egg-and-sugar mixture.

Put this in the top of a double boiler, stirring often. Do not let it boil! When it is thick enough to coat a spoon that has been withdrawn from the mixture, strain it into a bowl. Cool it, stirring from time to time.

When it begins to thicken whip the heavy cream, and add it along with the confectioners' sugar and vanilla sugar to the cooled mixture.

NOTE: If the sauce does not thicken, add 1 to 2 (4 to 5) Tbsp. of cornstarch mixed with a small amount of milk and reheat.

Ouzo or Pernod
Greek Cheese Turnovers
Greek Salad
Fresh Figs
Fenikia Cookies

•

This is an excellent menu for a vegetarian lunch. The flaky phyllo pastry can be purchased in sheets (in many grocery or gourmet shops) so that making the turnovers is a simple matter.

You might prefer a Greek wine served as an aperitif to the very unusual licorice flavor of Ouzo and Pernod—both of which turn milky when poured over ice.

Dessert can be casual if you keep the syrup warm in a fondu pot and let guests dip their cookies into the lemon and cinnamon flavored liquid.

GREEK CHEESE TURNOVERS

The Greek name for these is 'Tiropetes.'

Ingredients	6 Portions	24 Portions
Phyllo leaves	1 package	4 packages
Butter, melted	½ cup	2 cups
FILLING		
Feta Cheese	1 lb.	4 lb.
Eggs, slightly heaten	2 large	8 large
Sugar	½ cup	2 cups
White pepper	¼ tsp.	1 tsp.
Salt	Pinch	¼ tsp.

Preheat oven to 375°F.

In a large bowl, push cheese through a sieve. Mix well with eggs, sugar, pepper and salt. Set aside.

Take phyllo from refrigerator. Stack the phyllo and cover with a damp towel. Using one leaf at a time, brush with melted butter, then cut lengthwise in even strips 3 to 4 inches wide.

Place one tablespoon of filling at the bottom of each strip and fold up, flag-fashion, to make a triangle. Tuck last fold under, sealing with melted butter.

Place, seam-side down, 2 inches apart, on an ungreased cookie sheet. Brush with melted butter, and bake 10 to 15 minutes, or until golden brown.

GREEK SALAD

Great for dieters and vegetarians.

Ingredients	6 Portions	24 Portions
DRESSING		
Oil	3 Tbsp.	¾ cup
Vinegar	2 tsp.	2 Tbsp. + 2 tsp.
Sugar	1 Tbsp.	¼ cup
Salt	¼ tsp.	1 tsp.
Mustard, dry	⅛ tsp.	½ tsp.
Paprika	⅛ tsp.	½ tsp.
Celery seed	⅛ tsp.	½ tsp.
Garlic clove	1 small	4
SALAD		
Tomatoes, cut in wedges	3 large	2
Cucumbers, peeled & diced	2 medium	8

233

Green pepper, diced	¼	1
Onion, diced	½	2 small
Kalmato olives	¼ lb.	1 lb.
Salt	½ tsp.	2 tsp.
Oregano	½ tsp.	2 tsp.
Feta cheese, crumbled, optional		

DRESSING: Combine oil, vinegar, sugar, salt, dry mustard, paprika, celery seed and garlic clove in jar; shake well. Refrigerate 2 hours.

SALAD: Mix together in a salad bowl, tomatoes, cucumber, green pepper, onion and olives. Sprinkle with salt and oregano.

Remove garlic clove from dressing. Pour dressing on salad. Toss well. Add Feta cheese, if desired.

FENIKIA

The cookies are dipped in a lemon-cinnamon syrup then rolled in nuts.

Ingredients	2½ Dozen	9½ Dozen
Flour, sifted	1¾ cup	7 cups
Baking powder	1¼ tsp	1 Tbsp. + 2 tsp.
Margarine	1 stick	4 sticks
Sugar	¼ cup	1 cup
Soy oil	¼ cup + 2 Tbsp.	1½ cups
Orange juice	¼ cup	1 cup
Walnuts, ground	½ cup	2 cups
SYRUP		
Sugar	⅓ cup	1⅓ cups
Cinnamon	1 tsp.	1 Tbsp. + 1 tsp.
Water	¼ cup	1 cup
Corn syrup	¼ cup	1 cup
Lemon juice	2 tsp.	2 Tbsp. + 2 tsp.

Sift flour and baking powder together; set aside.
Stir margarine and sugar together. Add oil; beat until blended. Stir in orange juice. Gradually mix in sifted flour mixture until soft dough forms.
Shape into 1-inch balls. (Stir dough occasionally during shaping.)
Place on ungreased baking sheet. Bake in 350°F (moderate) oven 20 minutes or until lightly bowned. Remove from baking sheet and cool on wire rack.

SYRUP: Mix sugar, cinnamon, water, corn syrup and lemon juice together in medium saucepan. Bring to a boil over medium heat, stirring constantly. Boil 5 minutes. For coating cookies, reduce heat and keep syrup simmering.

When cookies are cool, with a slotted spoon, lower a few cookies at a time into syrup. Stir to coat evenly. Allow cookies to remain in syrup for 1 minute. Remove and place on wire rack to drain excess, then roll in ground walnuts. Allow cookies to dry completely.

Store in airtight container. Cookies may be baked in advance, stored and dipped in syrup as needed.

Store syrup in covered container in refrigerator. To reuse syrup, heat over low heat, stirring constantly.

Pâté Slice with Cornichon
Seafood Brioche
Tossed Endive with Lemon
Fresh Plum Tart

•

You can purchase beautiful pâtés, canned or fresh. Serve each slice on a leaf of Boston lettuce and garnish with tiny sour pickles.

Individual brioche will make charming little casseroles, if you cut off the tops and hollow them out to hold the scallop and shrimp mixture, flavored with brandy.

Leaves of Belgian endive, tossed with salt, freshly ground pepper and freshly squeezed lemon juice make a delightful salad.

SEAFOOD BRIOCHE

Serve the seafood mixture in individual brioche as small casseroles, or make larger brioche to hold four to eight portions.

Ingredients	8 Portions	24 Portions
Scallops	12	36
Thyme sprigs	2	6
Parsley sprigs	4	12
Dry white wine	2 cups	6 cups
Fish stock	1 cup	3 cups
Salt	To taste	To taste
Pepper, freshly ground	To taste	To taste
Prawns, jumbo, unshelled	2 lb.	6 lb.
Shrimp, shelled	10 oz.	2 lb.
Butter	½ cup	1½ cups
Shallots	8	24
Brandy or Calvados	½ cup	1½ cup
Flour, all-purpose	6 Tbsp.	1 cup + 2 Tbsp.
Heavy cream	1 cup	1 pint + 1 cup
Brioche (see Index)	8 individual or 2 large	24 individual or 6 large

Remove edible portion of each scallop, discarding the black thread and membrane. Wash under cold, running water. Place in saucepan with the thyme, parsley, white wine and fish stock. Season with salt and pepper.

Bring slowly to a boil and simmer for 7 to 8 minutes, then strain and reserve stock. Cut the scallops into large cubes.

Peel the prawns and shrimp. Heat the butter in a frying pan and add the finely chopped shallots. Cook until soft. Do not allow to burn. Add the prawns and shrimp. Cook until firm; then pour on the brandy and flame.

Sprinkle the flour over the seafood and mix. Moisten this roux with the reserved scallop stock.

Cook gently for 2 to 3 minutes, stirring continually, then add the cream and scallops. Cook for another 3 to 4 minutes. Do not allow to boil.

Cut a lid off the brioche and carefully scoop out the center. Place the loaf in 300°F oven for 10 to 15 minutes to heat through.

Just before serving, fill the brioche(s) with the seafood mixture and replace the lid(s). Serve immediately.

FRESH PLUM TART

Uncooked plums, glazed with marmalade, cover a rich creamy base.

Ingredients	1 Tart	3 Tarts
Cream cheese	**1 pkg. (8 oz.)**	**3 pkg. (8 oz. ea.)**
Sugar	¼ cup	¾ cup
Orange juice concentrate or **Cointreau**	3 Tbsp.	½ cup + 1 Tbsp.
Whipping cream	½ cup	1½ cups
Orange marmalade	½ cup	1½ cups
Plums, sliced	6	18

With an electric mixer, beat together cream cheese, sugar, orange juice or Cointreau; mixture should be smooth. Gradually add whipping cream, beating on medium speed until fluffy. Spread in a cooled, baked tart shell (recipe follows). Chill.

Heat orange marmalade, strain, and cool to lukewarm. Slice plums and arrange over the chilled filling. Brush marmalade over the fruit, making a thin even coating.

TART SHELL

Ingredients	1 Shell	3 Shells
Flour, sifted	**1 cup**	**3 cups**
Confectioners' sugar	**2 Tbsp.**	**6 Tbsp.**
Butter or margarine	**½ cup**	**1½ cup**

Preheat oven to 425°F.

Sift flour once and then again with sugar added. With pastry blender, cut in butter or margarine until mixture forms fine crumbs. Press dough over bottom and sides of a 10 or 11-inch flan pan or over the bottom and an inch up the sides of a 10 or 11-inch cheesecake pan (one with removable bottom or spring-release sides).

Bake for 8 to 10 minutes, or until lightly browned; cool before filling.

Plum Wine or Sake
Japanese Cocktail Crackers
Flank Steak Teriyaki
Japanese-Style Vegetables
Rice
Fortune Cookies
Grape Clusters on Lemon Leaves
Tiffin Tea Liqueur

•

Plum wine is a trifle on the sweet side. If that doesn't appeal to your taste, warm a bit of sake to serve with the Japanese Cocktail Crackers, or serve Japanese beer.

Beef is expensive in Japan and sparingly served. Flank Steak Teriyaki is made by marinating a less expensive cut of meat, then weaving thin strips of it onto skewers and broiling. The Japanese-Style Vegetables served with the steak are available frozen; or any combination of vegetables can be stir-fried.

Fortune Cookies aren't authentically Japanese, but they are fun to make when you're having guests because you can plant the fortunes inside and make them as outrageous as your guests will tolerate.

FLANK STEAK TERIYAKI

Marinate to tenderize and flavor steak strips before weaving them on skewers.

Ingredients	6 Portions	24 Portions
Flank steak	2 lb.	8 lb.
Soy sauce	¼ cup	1 cup
Garlic clove, minced	1	4
Soy oil	2 Tbsp.	½ cup
Ground ginger	1 tsp.	1 Tbsp. + 1 tsp.
Sugar	1 tsp.	1 Tbsp. + 1 tsp.

Trim any excess fat from steak. Cut into thin slices, about ⅛ inch wide, cutting long pieces in half. Place in shallow pan. Combine soy sauce, garlic, oil, ginger and sugar; pour over meat in pan. Let stand 1 hour.

Weave marinated steak strips onto bamboo or metal skewers. (For rare steak, push folds of meat close together on skewers; for well-done steak, push folds apart.) Place on rack in shallow pan. Broil for 5 to 8 minutes on each side.

FORTUNE COOKIES

Surprise your friends with tailor-made fortunes.

Ingredients	8 Cookies	24 Cookies
Cake flour, sifted	¼ cup	¾ cup
Sugar	2 Tbsp.	6 Tbsp.
Cornstarch	1 Tbsp.	3 Tbsp.
Salt	Dash	⅛ tsp.
Soy oil	2 Tbsp.	6 Tbsp.
Egg white	1	3
Water	1 Tbsp.	3 Tbsp.

Sift together flour, sugar, cornstarch, and salt. Add oil and egg white; stir until smooth. Add water; mix well.

Make one cookie at a time by pouring 1 Tbsp. of the batter on lightly greased skillet or griddle; spread to 3½-inch circle. Cook over low heat about 4 minutes or until lightly browned. Turn with wide spatula; cook 1 minute more.

Working quickly, place cookie on pot holder. Put paper strip printed with fortune in center; fold cookie in half and then fold again over edge of bowl. Place in muffin pan to cool.

INDIA

Dahl Soup
Chicken Korma
Sliced Tomatoes/Onion Rings
Fresh Green Chilis/Fresh Mint
Paratha
Carrot Halva

•

There are hundreds, or even thousands, of curry variations cooked in India every day. The word "curry" simply means, "sauce"; it can be mild or pungent, but will always be aromatic. Our recipe calls for dehydrated onion flakes because they are more like the low-water onions of India.

This American version of the Dahl Soup is made using condensed pea soup and chicken broth. The real Dahl Rasam is made using coconut water and split peas, and is flavored with fenugreek seed, cumin, mustard and lemon juice.

The dessert, Carrot Halva, is really a carrot pudding with raisins and two kinds of nuts—almonds and pistachios.

DAHL SOUP

Also excellent as an appetizer for an India dinner.

Ingredients	6 Portions	24 Portions
Whole black peppercorns	10	40
Whole cloves	10	40
Condensed pea soup	2 cans (11½ oz. ea.)	8 cans (11½ oz. ea.)
Condensed chicken broth	1 can (10¾ oz.)	4 cans (10¾ oz.)
Water	2 soup cans	8 soup cans
Ground turmeric	½ tsp.	2 tsp.

Tie black pepper and cloves in cheesecloth.

In a large saucepan combine pea soup, chicken broth and water. Bring to boiling point. Stir in turmeric; add whole spices.

Reduce heat and simmer, covered, for 30 minutes. Remove whole spices.

Serve garnished with croutons and parsley flakes, if desired.

CHICKEN KORMA

Tender chicken, pungent with curry, served over rice.

Ingredients	4 Portions	24 Portions
Onion flakes	⅓ cup	2 cups
Instant minced garlic	½ tsp.	1 Tbsp.
Water	¼ cup	1½ cup
Butter or margarine	2 Tbsp.	¾ cup
Soy oil	2 Tbsp.	¾ cup
Chicken, cut into eighths	3 lb.	18 lb.
Curry powder	2 Tbsp.	¾ cup
Ground turmeric	½ tsp.	1 Tbsp.
Black pepper, freshly ground	⅛ tsp.	¾ tsp.
Bay leaf	1	6
Yogurt, plain	½ cup	3 cups
Salt	1 tsp.	1 Tbsp.
Steamed rice	4 cups	24 cups

Rehydrate onion flakes and minced garlic in water for 10 minutes.

In a large skillet heat butter and oil. Add chicken, a few pieces at a time; brown on both sides; remove and set aside. Add rehydrated onion and garlic along with curry powder, turmeric, black pepper and bay leaf; cook and stir for 3 minutes.

Remove from heat and stir in yogurt and salt. Add browned chicken pieces, spooning some of the sauce over the chicken.

Simmer, covered, until chicken is fork-tender, about 35 minutes.

Arrange chicken on a heated platter over steamed rice. Remove excess fat from sauce; spoon over chicken. If desired, sprinkle with coconut.

PARATHA

Since it is folded three times, and oiled with each fold, the layers separate and flake as it fries.

Ingredients	16 Pieces	32 Pieces
All-purpose flour	1 cup + ½ cup for dusting	2 cups + 1 cup for dusting
Whole wheat flour	2 cups	4 cups
Vegetable shortening	3 Tbsp.	⅓ cup
Salt	1 tsp.	2 tsp.
Water, as needed	1 to 1½ cups	2 to 3 cups
Shortening, melted for brushing	¼ cup	½ cup

Combine 1 (2) cup all-purpose flour plus the whole wheat flour in a bowl. Rub shortening into it. Add salt. Add water, little by little, until the dough is firm and can be kneaded.

Place the dough on a marble or wooden board and knead for 10 to 15 minutes. This will be a very soft and pliable dough. Cover with a towel and let the dough rest for at least half an hour.

The dough can be made a day ahead and refrigerated. Remove from refrigerator about 30 minutes before you are ready to roll it out.

Knead the dough again for a minute and divide into two equal portions. Roll each into a cylinder and cut into 8 (16) equal parts. Roll the small pieces into smooth balls.

Working one at a time, place the ball on the work board, dust it generously with flour and roll into a 5-inch disc. Brush the top with shortening and fold in half. Brush the top of the semi-circle with shortening and fold in half again. You will now have a triangle-shaped dough.

Roll this out to about 6 or 7-inch triangle. These can be prepared about an hour ahead of time as long as they are covered with a sheet of plastic or a damp towel to prevent the dough from drying out.

When ready to fry the bread, heat an ungreased cast iron griddle for a moment or two. Put one bread at a time onto the griddle and cook for two minutes over medium heat until the bottom is cooked and brown spots appear. Flip the bread upside down with a pancake turner and cook the other side for a moment.

Meanwhile, brush the cooked side with shortening and flip the bread again. Cook a minute, then flip again and brush the top with shortening.

Keep warm and covered, and repeat with remaining triangles of bread. Serve hot.

CARROT HALVA

Really a spicy carrot pudding, crunchy with nuts.

Ingredients	8 Portions	24 Portions
Tender young carrots	1½ lb.	4½ lb.
Milk	2 quarts	6 quarts
Honey	2 Tbsp.	6 Tbsp.
Saffron	¹/₁₆ tsp.	¼ tsp.
Ground cinnamon	½ tsp.	1½ tsp.
Whole cardamoms, crushed	2	6
Sugar	1½ cup	4½ cups
Salt	1 tsp.	1 Tbsp.
Butter	5 Tbsp.	15 Tbsp.
Raisins	¼ cup	¾ cup
Almonds, toasted, chopped	To garnish	To garnish
Pistachios, chopped	To garnish	To garnish
SWEETENED WHIPPED CREAM		
Heavy cream	1 pint	3 pints
Sugar	¼ cup	¾ cup
Orange flower water	1 Tbsp.	3 Tbsp.

Dice carrots coarsely; add 1 quart (3 quarts) milk and blend in electric blender (or grate carrots on a fine grater and combine with milk).

Scald remaining milk in a large skillet. Add carrot mixture; boil 15 minutes. Stir in honey, saffron, cinnamon, cardamoms, sugar, salt, 4 Tbsp. (12 Tbsp.) butter and raisins. Lower heat and simmer until mixture is almost dry (about 1 hour).

Add remaining 1 Tbsp. (3 Tbsp.) butter; heat 10 more minutes until all moisture is absorbed. Chill 4 to 5 hours.

Whip cream until stiff. Garnish with whipped cream, almonds and pistachios.

Dutch Beer
Oysters on the Half Shell
Stuffed Breast of Veal
Hot Curried Slaw
Toasted Rusk
Dutch Apple Pie

•

A meat loaf mixture, flavored with beer, is rolled inside the veal breast before it goes into the Dutch oven for browning.

Hot Curried Slaw is an unusual vegetable dish which joins the veal in the oven for 15 minutes while guests are enjoying their icy oysters.

The hot Dutch Apple Pie is even more irresistible served with whipped cream flavored with almond or with lemon rind.

DUTCH BREAST OF VEAL

Veal with a stuffing of ground beef and pork.

Ingredients	6 Portions	24 Portions
POACHING STOCK		
Veal bone sawed into 2-inch lengths	2	8
Water	To cover	To cover
Onions, coarsely chopped	½ cup	2 cups
Celery, coarsely chopped with leaves	½ cup	2 cups
Whole black peppercorns	6	24
Bay leaf	1 small	4
Parsley, chopped	½ cup	2 cups
STUFFING		
White bread, fresh	2 slices	8 slices
Beer	⅓ cup	1⅓ cups
Butter	1 tsp.	1 Tbsp. + 1 tsp.
Onions, chopped	½ cup	2 cups
Beef, ground	½ lb.	2 lb.
Pork, ground	½ lb.	2 lb.
Eggs, lightly beaten	1	4
Parsley, finely chopped	3 Tbsp.	¾ cup
Nutmeg, ground	⅛ tsp.	½ tsp.
Salt	To taste	To taste
Black pepper, freshly ground	To taste	To taste
Veal breasts, boned and trimmed	1 breast (4–4½ lb.)	4 breasts
Lard	3 Tbsp.	¾ cup

In a heavy 3- to 4-quart saucepan, bring the veal bones and water to a boil over high heat, skimming off any foam and scum that rise to the surface.

Add the onions, celery, peppercorns, bay leaves and parsley; reduce the heat to low and partially cover the pan. Simmer, undisturbed for 1 hour.

Strain the stock through a fine sieve set over a bowl, discarding the bones, vegetables and spices. Set the stock aside.

Tear the slices of bread into small pieces and soak in beer; gently squeeze them and set them aside in a large mixing bowl.

In a skillet, melt butter over moderate heat. When the foam subsides add onions and cook, stirring frequently, for 5 minutes, or until they are soft and transparent.

Scrape the contents of the skillet into the bowl with the bread, and add the beef, pork, egg, parsley, nutmeg, half of the salt and a few grindings of pepper.

Knead the mixture with your hands or beat with a large spoon until all the ingredients are well-blended.

Preheat the oven to 325°F.

Place the veal flat side down on a board or table, sprinkle with remaining salt and a few grindings of pepper and, with a knife or spatula, spread the ground-meat stuffing mixture evenly over the veal.

Beginning with a wide side, roll up the veal jelly-roll fashion into a thick cylinder. Tie the roll at both ends and in the center with kitchen cord.

In a heavy casserole just large enough to hold the roll comfortably, melt the lard over high heat. Add the veal roll and brown evenly on all sides. Pour in reserved stock and bring to a boil over high heat.

Cover the casserole and transfer to the middle of the oven. Cook for 1¾ hours, turning the roll over after the first hour. Then remove the cover and cook, basting occasionally with the pan juices, for 30 minutes longer.

HOT CURRIED SLAW

Excellent served with veal, ham or pork prepared almost any way.

Ingredients	6 Portions	24 Portions
Cabbage, shredded	6 cups	24 cups
Stock	2 cups	½ gallon
Onion, instant minced	2 Tbsp.	½ cup
Salt	1½ tsp.	2 Tbsp.
Garlic, instant minced	¼ tsp.	1 tsp.
Ground black pepper	¼ tsp.	1 tsp.
Bay leaves	1 small	4
Whole cloves	1	4
Butter or margarine	3 Tbsp.	¾ cup
Flour	4 Tbsp.	1 cup
Curry powder	1 Tbsp.	¼ cup
Light cream or milk, heated	1½ cups	1½ quarts
Ground nuts, or fine bread crumbs	¼ cup	1 cup

Preheat oven to 425°F.

Combine cabbage, stock, minced onion, salt, minced garlic and black pepper in a large pot. Tie bay leaves and cloves in cheesecloth; add to pot. Bring to boiling point. Reduce heat, cover and cook for 10 minutes. Remove spice bag.

247

Melt butter in a large skillet. Stir in flour and curry powder. Cook 2 minutes. Gradually pour in cream, stirring constantly. Cook until smooth and thickened. Pour over cabbage mixture, blending thoroughly. (Correct seasoning if necessary).

Turn mixture into greased baking pans. Sprinkle with nuts. Bake for 15 minutes.

DUTCH APPLE PIE

A streusel-topped pie baked in a brown paper bag.

Ingredients	One 9-Inch Pie	Three 9-Inch Pies
Pie shell, unbaked with		
upstanding fluted rim	1 9-inch	3 9-inch
Brown paper bag	1 large	3 large
Golden delicious apples, or		
other cooking apples, cubed,		
peeled, cored	6 cups	18 cups
Sugar	½ cup	1½ cups
Flour	2 Tbsp.	6 Tbsp.
Nutmeg	¼ tsp.	¾ tsp.
TOPPING		
Flour	½ cup	1½ cups
Sugar	½ cup	1½ cups
Butter or margarine	¼ lb.	¾ lb.

To prepare the bag, place the bottom of a 9-inch pie plate over the middle of one side and mark around the plate. Cut around the circle and reserve the cut-out.

In a large mixing bowl, combine sugar, flour and nutmeg.

Peel apples, core and cut in 1-inch cubes. Toss with sugar mixture until well-coated and turn into pie shell.

To make the streusel mixture, combine flour and sugar and cut in butter to make coarse crumbs. Sprinkle streusel over the top.

Place the pie in the center of the paper bag so the top is visible through the cutout. Fold over the ends of the bag in a drugstore fold and fasten with paper clips. Place bag on a large cookie sheet and place paper cutout back in place over the top of the pie.

Bake in a 400°F oven for about 30 minutes, then remove the paper cut-out and continue to bake about 30 minutes longer or until the apples are tender and the crust is browned. Remove pie from the bag. Serve warm, if desired.

Mediterranean Pâté

Cous-Cous

Olives, Scallions, Radishes

French Bread

Grapes and Apples with
a French goat-milk cheese such as
Bucheron or Montrachet

Algerian Tea

•

The pâté may not seem Algerian, but that country borders on the sea and uses shellfish and fish often. Serve the French bread with the pâté as an appetizer and let your guests spread apple wedges with the soft tangy cheese for dessert.

Finish the meal with the sweet fragrant tea. When no fresh orange blossoms are blooming outside your window, you can add a drop or two of orange water.

MEDITERRANIAN PÂTÉ

Garnish with whole, cooked prawns and lemon slices.

Ingredients	1 Pound	3 Pounds
Prawns, cooked or shrimp meat	½ lb.	1½ lb.
or	or	or
Shrimp broken and drained	2 cans (4½ oz.)	6 cans
Almonds, blanched, toasted and chopped	¼ cup	¾ cup
Ginger, candied and grated	1 Tbsp.	3 Tbsp.
Curry powder	½ tsp.	1½ tsp.
Garlic, mashed	1 clove	3 cloves
Lemon juice, fresh	1 Tbsp.	3 Tbsp.
Parsley, finely chopped	2 Tbsp.	⅓ cup
Butter, melted	2 Tbsp.	6 Tbsp.
Kalamata (Greek) olives, chopped	4	12
Bread, torn	½ cup	1½ cups
Salt	To taste	To taste
Pepper, freshly ground black	To taste	To taste

Puree prawns or shrimp in blender or food processor. Blend into smooth paste with remaining ingredients.

Form into a loaf; chill, preferably overnight.

COUS-COUS

The classic dish of North African cuisine.

Ingredients	6 Portions	24 Portions
Chick peas, canned	1 cup	4 cups
Faufel (see note)	2 cups	8 cups
Water	2 cups	½ gallon
Salt	1½ tsp.	⅓ cup
Butter or Margarine	½ lb.	2 lb.
Onions, chopped	2 cups	8 cups
Lamb, boneless, cubed	2 lb.	8 lb.
Chicken, disjointed	1 (5 lb.)	4 (5 lb. ea.)
Carrots, sliced	2	8
Green peppers, sliced	2	8
Tomatoes, peeled & cubed	3	12
Black pepper, ground	1 tsp.	1 Tbsp. + 1 tsp.
Cayenne pepper	¼ tsp.	1 tsp.

Yellow squash, cubed	1 cup	4 cups
Green peas, fresh and shelled, or frozen	1 lb.	4 lb.

Put the faufal in a bowl and stir in the water and 1 (3) tsp. of salt. Rub mixture between the hands about 1 foot above the bowl, letting it fall into the bowl. Do this several times. Do not allow lumps to form. Let faufal soak until all the water is absorbed.

Melt half the butter/margarine in a Dutch oven or large saucepan and brown the onions, lamb, and chicken. Add boiling water to reach half-way up the ingredients. Mix in the carrots, green peppers, tomatoes, black pepper, cayenne pepper, and remaining salt.

Turn the faufal into a large strainer or colander and place over the saucepan. Cover as tightly as possible. Cook over low heat 1½ hours.

To chicken mixture add the squash, green peas and chick peas. Replace colander, cover and continue cooking 45 minutes longer, or until chicken is tender.

Stir remaining butter or margarine into faufal with a fork. Heap the faufal in the center of a platter with the chicken, lamb, vegetables and sauce around it.

NOTE: Faufal consists of tiny pellets of wheat. It can be found in Near Eastern or Oriental food shops. You may substitute cracked wheat, wheat semolina or even farina.

ALGERIAN TEA

A very sweet, mint tea, best made with fresh spearmint.

Ingredients	6 Portions	24 Portions
Green tea	4 tsp.	⅓ cup
Honey	6 Tbsp.	1½ cup
Fresh spearmint leaves, firmly packed	1¼ cups	5 cups
Water, boiling	4 cups	16 cups

Combine ingredients and allow tea to steep at least 3 minutes. Stir slightly and correct for sweetness. Serve hot in glasses.

Fresh orange blossoms can be added to the pot before pouring in the boiling water.

Tostadas Broiled with Cheese
Chimechangas with Beef and Bean Filling
Tomato and Green Chili Relish
Mixed Green Salad
Mango Sherbet
Sangria

•

It's easy to understand why Mexican food has become so popular; it's not difficult to prepare and fairly inexpensive, even if you have to buy a few special items such as chilis.

One of the nice things about Chimechangas is that they can be prepared ahead and frozen. You don't have to make your own tortillas; they're available frozen or canned. You can even buy refried beans in a can.

When mangos are out of season, any sherbet can be used to cool the fire.

CHIMECHANGAS

Crisp, brown, deliciously filled packages.

Ingredients	6 Portions	24 Portions
BEEF AND BEAN FILLING		
Salad oil	1 Tbsp.	¼ cup
Ground beef, lean	¾ lb.	3 lb.
Onion, chopped	1 large	4 large
Green pepper, chopped	1	4
Garlic, minced	1 clove	4 cloves
Salt	½ tsp.	2 tsp.
Cumin, ground	½ tsp.	2 tsp.
Chili powder	2 Tbsp.	½ cup
Cayenne pepper	⅛ tsp.	½ tsp.
Refried beans	½ cup	2 cups
Jack cheese, grated	1 cup (4 oz.)	4 cups (1 lb.)
Flour tortillas	1 dozen	4 dozen
Salad oil	As needed	As needed
Guacamole dip, frozen and thawed	2 cans	8 cans
Tomato and Green Chili Relish (see recipe below)		
Sour cream	1½ cups	6 cups

Heat salad oil in a large frying pan. Add ground beef, stirring to break up meat; cook until lightly browned. Add onion, green pepper, and garlic; cook, stirring, until onion is transparent.

Stir in salt, ground cumin, chili powder, cayenne and refried beans. Cook, stirring constantly, over medium-low heat until hot. Fold in shredded jack cheese and set aside to cool.

Place about ¼ cup of filling near center of each tortilla. Fold tortilla around filling, tucking in sides, fasten with wooden picks.

If tortillas are too brittle to roll, lightly dampen with water, wrap in foil and heat in a 350°F oven until warm and pliable.

To fry, pour salad oil ¾-inch deep into a large frying pan; place over medium-high heat until it reaches 370°F on a deep-fat frying thermometer. Fry 3 or 4 chimechangas at a time, turning as needed, until browned, about 1½ minutes.

Remove with tongs, drain on paper towels, and keep warm if you plan to serve them right away.

If made ahead, cool thoroughly, cover, and freeze. To reheat, place frozen chimechangas in a single layer in a shallow rimmed pan; bake uncovered about 25 minutes or until hot.

Serve with *Tomato and Green Chili Relish* and sour cream.

TOMATO AND GREEN CHILI RELISH

A sauce to serve with Chimechangas.

Ingredients	6 Portions	24 Portions
Tomatoes, peeled and diced	1 lb.	4 lb.
Green chilis, diced	4 oz.	1 lb.
Onion, chopped	½ cup	2 cups
White vinegar	1 Tbsp.	¼ cup
Sugar	1 tsp.	1 Tbsp. + 1 tsp.
Salt	1 tsp.	1 Tbsp. + 1 tsp.
Pepper	¼ tsp.	1 tsp.

Combine tomatoes, green chilis, onion, vinegar, sugar and salt and pepper. Mix well, cover, and refrigerate.

MANGO SHERBET

Three medium-sized mangoes will make half a gallon.

Ingredients	½ Gallon	2 Gallons
Sugar, granulated	1 cup	4 cups
Water	3 cups	12 cups
Mangoes, fresh puree	3 cups	12 cups
Lemon juice, fresh	4 Tbsp.	1 cup
Egg whites, stiffly beaten	3	12

In a saucepan, combine sugar and water. Boil for 5 minutes. Cool.

Combine mango puree, lemon juice, and sugar syrup. (To puree mangoes, use electric blender on medium speed, a food processor, or mash with potato masher.) Add stiffly beaten egg whites. Churn-freeze.

Index

259

263